Blessings ~

Carolyn R. Allen

4/22

Col. 1:28-29

# LIFE-CHANGING
## QUESTIONS

*Powerful Questions*
*for*
*Personal Growth and Ministry*

## Rev. Dr. Carolyn R. Allen

LIFE-CHANGING QUESTIONS
Copyright © 2022
Rev. Dr. Carolyn R. Allen

All Rights Reserved

PUBLISHED BY

Rev. Dr. Carolyn R. Allen, 1025 Vance Ave., Fort Wayne, IN 46805

SCRIPTURE SOURCES

*Unless otherwise noted, scripture references are from The Holy Bible, New American Standard Bible, (NY: Cambridge University Press, 2013).*

*The Holy Bible, New Living Translation, (Carol Stream, IL: Tyndale House Publishers, Inc., 1996, 2004, 2007, 2013, 2015).*

*The Holy Bible, The Message, (Carol Stream, IL: Tyndale House Publishers, Inc., © Eugene H. Peterson, 2002. UBP NavPress).*

*The NET Bible ©, (Biblical Studies Press, L.L.C., 2005, www.NETBIBLE.com).*

ISBN: (print): 978-1-66783-095-7
ISBN: (eBook): 978-1-66783-096-4

# CONTENTS

# ENDORSEMENTS

Pastor Carolyn Allen's *Life Changing Questions* is an important book in helping discover and refine one's destiny. The principles Pastor Carolyn presents in this book have been gleaned from many years of helping people learn to walk in freedom. *Life-Changing Questions* is a resource filled with helpful insights and practical tools for learning how to ask the right kinds of questions.

I have known Carolyn and her husband Ron for thirty-four years and have found them wise and passionate servants of Christ and His Church. Ron gave me one of the most important prophecies for my life to date, and I received the most powerful impartation of my life when he and Happy Leman laid hands on me at a Vineyard Regional meeting in October 1989. Carolyn is a wise pastor married to a wise pastor. They have been in leadership in the Vineyard and in the Anglican Communion of churches. I have great respect for their leadership, teaching, and writings.

Dr. Randy Clark
D.D., D. Min., Th.D., M.Div., B.S. Religious Studies
Overseer of the apostolic network of Global Awakening
President of Global Awakening Theological Seminary

Rev. Dr. Carolyn Allen has done the church a great service by her thoughtful, Biblical, and pragmatic work on *Life-Changing Questions*. The fruit of Dr. Carolyn's careful study and decades of practical experience makes this work a treasure for the believer who seeks greater discovery in personal growth and for every minister who desires greater effectiveness in pastoral care and healing ministry.

*Life-Changing Questions* is not a theoretical treatise. It is a practical, substantive, ministry tool based on thorough Biblical study and insightfully gleaned principles that, when applied, will lead to enduring fruitfulness in ministering wholeness in Jesus' name. The resources provided in the appendices alone can be employed for lengthy seasons of enrichment in one's personal journey into the abundant life promised by Jesus.

Thank you, Dr. Carolyn, for decades of faithful ministry and for sharing this labor of love with us to strengthen the Body of Christ.

The Rt. Rev. Mark A. Engel
Diocesan Bishop
Anglican Diocese of the Great Lakes

Now that I am officially an old(er) guy I quite often get asked the following question: "How do you walk with God for decades and maintain passion and purpose, intimacy and impact?" My answer is simple, as good answers to good questions always are: hunger and compassion - hunger for God and compassion for people. If you live at the crossroads of God's presence and people's pain, you will always see God.

Carolyn Allen has lived her life at that corner on her road trip through life and ministry. Her writings impart the joy, challenge, and wisdom one finds there. She has discovered *the power of questions* to create an atmosphere for *discovery* (finding God's truth) rather than *declaration* (being told truth). She has also learned to rest in the reality that "It is God Who is at work in you" and to enjoy the pleasure of watching God do His thing. *Life-Changing Questions* will invite and nudge you to spend more time at the crossroads of hunger and compassion.

Chip Judd
Pastor of Leadership Care
Seacoast Church

I avidly consumed this book cover to cover (including the essential appendices) in bite-size pieces. *Life-Changing Questions* is not a book I want you to simply read. It is a book I encourage you to experience. I found myself stopping at regular intervals for life-impacting encounters with God.

If you are ready to take a leap forward in your relationships with God and people, this insightful book is for you. Dr. Carolyn has skillfully put her years of experience on these pages to give us a practical way to draw close to God and be transformed by Him.

Linda Roeder, MCC
Co-Chairman
Restoring the Foundations Board of Directors

Rev. Carolyn Allen has always asked the most profound questions to me and to those who have sought her counsel. Learning to ask the right questions has led to greater freedom, maturity, secure identity and ultimately wholeness. Every time I meet with Rev. Carolyn, her insightful questions have an impact on me that changes me and helps me to hear Jesus better.

*Life-Changing Questions* is a powerful sequel to her book, *Journey into Wholeness*. It equips the reader with the right tools that lead us and those to whom we minister into greater wholeness. Carolyn is a dear friend and a trusted partner in pastoral care and healing ministry.

Fr. Keith Hartsell
Founder
Equipped to Heal Ministries

Carolyn teaches you the art of asking the Lord the right questions, then receiving and honoring His responses. I believe this process is the quickest way to healing, spiritual maturity, and anointed ministry. Take it to heart. Practice it!

Dr. Mark Virkler
Founder and President
Christian Leadership University

In her powerful and practical book, Rev. Dr. Carolyn R. Allen makes the bold statement, *"Questions determine the course of our lives."* Throughout each chapter, she carefully articulates the importance of asking questions on our journey – how we ask them and who we ask. She summarizes her challenge to us with a profound question: "Are our questions taking us on a path of discovery with the Holy Spirit, or on a path of self-condemnation, guilt and shame?"

Her insights are filled with wisdom and expertise that come from years spent years spent not only caring for others but also walking intimately with Jesus. As a fellow pastor of over forty years, I am convinced this is an indispensable guide to helping our people partner with the Holy Spirit in being fully transformed.

In addition to thorough chapters highlighted with real-life stories, there are six appendices that are jam packed with easy-to-use resources. Every person needs a copy of this book so all can experience what Carolyn has found to be 100% true: *Change your questions. Change your life.*

> Dianne Leman
> Founding Pastor
> The Vineyard Church of Central IL

Dr. Carolyn Allen provides an incredible resource to help us grow and mature in our relationship with the Creator of the universe. Her insights assist us in taking Romans 12:2 from words on a page to applying them to our own lives. Being transformed by the renewing of our minds is an incredible gift and an area in which we all need to continually work.

*Life-Changing Questions* helped convince me that changing our thoughts and learning how to ask discovery questions instead of condemning questions truly changes our lives.

> Mark A. Robison
> Chairman and President
> Brotherhood Mutual Insurance Company

*Life-Changing Questions* is a treasure of wisdom coming from decades of Carolyn Allen's fruitful ministry. Having worked with Carolyn for many years, I can say that much of my spiritual growth can be attributed to the truths found in this book. Not only have I grown because of it, but it has also helped equip me as a pastor to more effectively minster to others and enable them to approach Jesus, ask Him questions, and hear from Him directly. It is so refreshing to read a book knowing that every chapter has countless hours of real-life ministry experience behind it. I highly recommend *Life-Changing Questions* to help you grow in healthy dialogue with yourself, those around you, and Jesus Himself.

Rev. Dave Frincke
Senior Pastor, Heartland Church
United Adoration Movement Leader

*Life-Changing Questions* by Dr. Carolyn Allen is a thought-provoking treatise in teaching you how to more effectively choose the right questions to discover the real answers you need to navigate life and ministry more fruitfully. Over fifty years of pastoral experience are distilled into a focused way of exploring and discovering the most effective pathway to health and wholeness in pastoral care.

I highly recommend this book to all disciples of Jesus Christ who want to explore their understanding and application of biblical truth while sharpening their people-helping skills.

Rev. Canon Dr. Ronald D. Allen
Founding Pastor
Heartland Church

Let me immediately declare an interest; Carolyn Allen is one of my favourite people. She combines the unique gifting of being immediately trustworthy, comforting and wise, yet through a wonderful coaching style will not allow you to settle for anything less than your God-given potential.

This book embodies her character as it gently but firmly leads you through the key questions that can activate change. On one hand, like many life-changing books it shares the familiar. On the other hand, it offers profound insight.

Carolyn has long possessed the wisdom of a spiritual elder whilst at the same time being open to new insights and, of course, the leading of the Holy Spirit. She also makes the best fried eggs I have ever tasted!

As you can see, I am a fan of both her work and character. This book gives you the benefit of both. Who would not want that?

Rev. Gary Smith
Director, The Message Trust, UK

# AUTHOR'S NOTE

*"If you spend just an afternoon in conversation with Carolyn Allen, you will soon recognize her heart for people to have an encounter with the Father and His heart for us. The way she coaches people to get there with questions is completely life-changing!"*

Liam Graham, Associate Pastor, Heartland Church

This is a beautiful statement of why I wrote *Life-Changing Questions*. My hope and heart's desire are that the ideas presented will empower the reader's journey into transformation as they put into practice life-changing principles.

# EDITOR'S NOTE

When Dr. Carolyn Allen first asked me to consider editing *Life-Changing Questions*, I was more than happy to say yes. My soul and spirit had already experienced profound healing after going through SOULCARE ministry and applying the principles presented in her book *Journey into Wholeness*.

And then life continued and I found myself facing new challenges and pondering new questions — questions I couldn't properly articulate. So I embraced Carolyn's latest project with confident expectancy, and I was not disappointed. As we worked our way through each chapter, I found myself laughing, crying, experiencing the healing touch of the Holy Spirit, and connecting with the Lord more deeply than ever before.

The Lord of the universe earnestly desires for us to learn redemptive ways to interact with others and with Him. He cares infinitely about each detail of our lives, and He loves dialoguing with us and answering the questions in our hearts.

Applying the principles that Dr. Carolyn teaches and models for us is indeed life-changing. Learning to ask the right kinds of questions in redemptive ways will transform your relationships with your friends, coworkers, loved ones, and — most of all — the Lord Himself.

Janet Willig
Founder, Streams of Hope Christian Academy

# ACKNOWLEDGMENTS

Once again, I am indebted to Ron, my husband, best friend and partner in ministry for fifty-four years. He patiently waited for me to push the send button, putting this book into the hands of the designer and publisher. Thank you, Ron, for always believing in me and encouraging me to step out and do my best.

Thank you to Pastor Dave Frincke, the Heartland Church staff, pastoral care teammates, and church family who have prayed for me, encouraged me, and motivated me to write this book on questions. I'm not sure how many times I've heard this question over the last few months, "When is your book about questions going to be ready? We need it." You are all part of this journey with me as we learn how to ask better questions. Many have prayed. Some ministered alongside, helping develop the principles, while others read the manuscript and gave constructive feedback. Thank you!

I also appreciate all who have come to the pastoral care team to receive healing and hope. Your vulnerability and courage allowed us to deepen our understanding and practice of the power of question-centered ministry. May God continue to make you whole in body, soul and spirit as you journey with Him.

Thank you to those who have collaborated with me by sharing your God stories of how questions have impacted you. Many will be blessed as they catch a glimpse of your journey. Thank you for your contributions.

Many thanks to Janet Willig, who has sacrificially given of time and talent to edit this book. Three p.m. on Thursday afternoons has been a highlight of my week this past year as we met to revise, revise, revise. You corrected, challenged and encouraged me to work with excellence, no matter how often the work needed a do-over. I never knew how much an author needed to struggle over the choice of a single word! Thank you for teaching me as we worked on this project. I'm forever grateful.

Rev. Dr. Carolyn R. Allen
Author

# INTRODUCTION

*Questions determine the course of our lives.*

Does that sound like an unrealistic statement to you? Implausible? Too bold? Impractical? Unbelievable?

In high school, I heard a lecture on preparing for the future. The purpose of the speech was to provoke us to consider what we would do with our lives. Where would we go to school? What would we study? Would we travel? What were our dreams? Our goals? Three questions in particular that were presented have played an influential role in the course of my life:

- Who will be your Master?

- Who will be your mate?

- What will be your mission and message?

Life is full of questions. Asking questions causes us to ponder possibilities. The questions I referenced led me on a path of discovery, opening doors of opportunities beyond my wildest imaginations. However, some of our inner dialogue framed as questions can cause us to judge ourselves to the point of hindering a successful, joyful life.

I have worked in ministry environments all of my life. Caring for people's souls has been a rich training ground to observe that it makes a tremendous difference in a person's ability to make Godly choices when they learn how to ask discovery questions instead of condemning questions. It is critical to ask the right questions and to ask the Right Person at the right time. These principles facilitate healing of the soul – the mind, will, and emotions – resulting in transformation. At Heartland Church[1], we train a team known as SOULCARE to assist with pastoral care using these principles.

> AT TIMES, WE BECOME TRAPPED IN PAST EXPERIENCES AND FIND IT DIFFICULT TO MOVE INTO THE DESTINY GOD HAS DESIGNED FOR US.

At times, we become trapped in past experiences and find it difficult to move into the destiny God has designed for us. Many of us find ourselves stuck in our past because of unforgiveness, unhealed hurts and wounds, thought patterns that don't agree with God, and demonic interference. We can be hindered from living in freedom because of vows, bitter root judgments, curses, and ungodly soul ties. We don't like some of the behaviors and feelings we experience in our journey with Christ, but we don't know how to change. We keep trying. We do the things we know to do. But we are stuck. The SOULCARE team, assisted with an assessment and an interview with the participant, crafts a Holy Spirit-led ministry plan. The plan includes questions and anointed prayers that help get us unstuck so we can live in the present and move into the destiny God has designed for us.

For clarification as you read, I identify people trained to lead others through a transformation journey as ministry facilitators. People desiring prayer ministry are named participants.

We learn that if we don't like what we are experiencing in our lives now, we can – with God's help – **CHANGE OUR THOUGHTS AND CHANGE OUR LIVES!** I explored this and the SOULCARE ministry in *Journey into Wholeness*.[2] We ask the Lord many questions in this process as we learn how to refocus our thoughts to align with Him.

In *Life-Changing Questions*, I explore the power of asking questions, not only for ourselves but in our dialogue with others. While changing our thoughts can change our lives, learning to ask great questions facilitates Godly decisions about what ideas we will embrace. So I add another phrase to CHANGE OUR THOUGHTS AND CHANGE OUR LIVES...**CHANGE OUR QUESTIONS AND CHANGE OUR LIVES!**

Ask the right question.

Ask the Right Person.

Ask at the right time to discover God's path for your life.

Let's learn how together.

# CHAPTER ONE:

## *Overview*

QUESTIONS ARE A PART OF EVERYDAY LIFE. IF WE pay attention to our inner dialogue, a good portion of it is questions. Inner dialogues are the conversations we have with ourselves. These questions start the moment we begin our day: What time is it? Why do I have to get up? Do I have to go to work today? Shall I shower today? Wash my hair? What shall I wear? Will I be on time? What is my first appointment?

Why do I look this way? Why didn't I go to bed earlier last night? What is wrong with me this morning? What kind of mood will my boss be in today? What will happen in the meeting today? What will go wrong today? What will go right today? What possibilities will open up for me today? What am I looking forward to today? What am I dreading today? What will I eat for breakfast this morning?

As we entertain this inner dialogue, we begin to take the actions we need to get moving for the day. Note that before we take the steps, our inner dialogue consists of questions. Some questions lead to taking action, some change how we think about others or ourselves, and some are rhetorical. Some have the answers embedded in them. Some are designed to motivate, some to ponder.

As mentioned in the introduction, this book explores the power of asking questions for ourselves, in our dialogue with others, and most importantly, in our dialogue with God. How can we know when to ask a question? How can we know what to ask next? What is the purpose of the questions, how can we learn to frame them, and how can we keep connected to God – or keep another person connected to God instead of us as ministry facilitators? Ministry teammates began to bombard me with these questions.

These conversations started me on a journey thinking about the importance and the nature of questions. I looked at how Jesus used questions in the Gospels in different ways with varying results. We can learn from His example. What questions did He ask, how did He frame them, and what goal did He have in mind for the hearer(s)? These are all points to ponder and learn from to gain applicable truth for life's challenges. Even our enemy uses basic questions meant to rob us of our eternal destiny. What do you think are the results of his questions?

I have learned there are different ways to ask the same question that connect with different people. Some ways keep us in negativity and on a path to self-condemnation. Others elevate us to a Kingdom of God perspective and a discovery path with the Holy Spirit leading and guiding. Can we learn to shift from one to the other by asking better questions? What are some life-changing questions we can all ask ourselves to process our thoughts, start us on a path to discovery, and help us establish new ways of thinking?

How can we frame questions that will enable people to learn skills to change their lives? What are some life-changing questions we can all use?

Bottom line – how can we become more effective – in our personal lives and ministry – by asking the right questions to the Right Person? What safeguards can we have in place to protect us from using questions to manipulate or control people? What motivation drives our questions? Can we become a community of faith that is intentional about asking questions as a lifestyle – questions that direct our attention to the Lord and cause us to reframe our thinking to agree with God?

# WE CANNOT BELIEVE EVERYTHING WE THINK!

I am convinced that *we cannot believe everything we think*! There is a desperate need in our culture to learn how to evaluate our thought processes and replace the ones that produce ungodly fruit. Our behavior reveals what thoughts we have embraced and what we believe to be true. *Beliefs drive emotions that result in actions.* Some are Godly, and some are not. How can we use questions to make a path for discovery led by the Holy Spirit to produce Godly fruit? Our Heavenly Father desires our transformation into His Son's nature and character (2 Corinthians 3:18).

We have been given the power to make these choices by our Creator. As we learn to change the questions we ask, we choose different thoughts and become more fruitful. A question not asked is a door not opened;[3] a possibility not explored; a potential not realized; a discovery not discovered; a connection with the Divine not made.

Albert Einstein is quoted as saying, "If I had an hour to solve a problem and my life depended on the solution, I would spend the first fifty-five minutes determining the proper question to ask for once I know the proper question, I could solve the problem in less than five minutes."[4]

Asking questions that will lead us to a dialogue with the Holy Spirit, our teacher and guide (John 14:26), opens the door to multiple God-opportunities. When we spend time with Him asking questions and listening to His wisdom, we find a foundation from which to live. I have named this process PAL, which is an acronym for Pause, Ask, Listen. You will see PAL frequently used throughout this book.

# PAL: PAUSE, ASK, LISTEN

PAL is simply what the acronym states:

- *Pause:* create a space where you can be alone to have a conversation with the Lord.

- *Ask:* Determine the question you want to ask the Lord and write it down. What is troubling you? What is the challenge or issue for which you need help? Once you have asked the question,

- *Listen:* When you ask a question, it is valuable to take time to listen for the answer. It would be rude to ask the Creator of the Universe a question and walk off without waiting for His response. Listen and record what you hear.

We are privileged as followers of Jesus Christ to have a God who loves to speak to His children. He desires a personal relationship with each one of us and loves to have conversations with us. He wants us to know Him. "This is eternal life – that they may know God" (John 17:3). John 10:27 says, "My sheep hear My voice."

Sometimes we are too busy and don't take time to be quiet to hear His voice. Some people don't know that God wants to talk to them. And some have been hearing His voice but haven't recognized it.

Others have never been taught how to hear God's voice. After many agonizing years of seeking someone who could teach him how to hear God's voice, Dr. Mark Virkler learned this: "God's voice sounds like spontaneous flowing thoughts which light upon your mind while your eyes are fixed on Jesus. Hearing Him speak to you is as simple as quieting yourself down, fixing your eyes on Jesus, tuning to spontaneity and writing: Stillness – Vision – Spontaneity – Journaling."[5]

Meditate on what you hear. Continue to ask questions about what you hear. Keep the dialogue moving and listen for the heart of the Lord as you develop a conversational style with Him. When you don't understand what you hear, ask for clarification. The Lord never gets tired of talking with us.

PAL is an intentional activation that can become part of your daily routines. You can PAL at the grocery, the hairdresser's, and in the middle of a conversation – whenever you need wisdom.

I want to strongly emphasize at the outset of this book that using the PAL activation to connect with and hear truth from the Lord requires using principles to discern and confirm that it is indeed the Lord speaking. There are times I'm not sure if what I have heard is God speaking to me. There are also times I listen to people in a ministry setting say what they think the Lord has just spoken, and I know it doesn't agree with a Biblical principle. It doesn't reflect the character and nature of our God. Rather than shut them down, I have an opportunity to teach them about the importance of testing what they hear.

It is helpful to have them say this: "Lord, I thought I heard You say _____ (repeat what they said). I'm not sure that is right. Was that really You?" Sometimes hearing the words out loud helps people recognize that what they thought they heard wasn't from God. Another phrase I use is, "This doesn't sound/feel quite right to me. Could you tell me a Scripture or a story from the Bible that illustrates that thought?" If they can't come up with one right then, it becomes an assignment to search the Scriptures before we meet again. They can PAL, "Lord, I'm not sure this is You. Could You lead me to Scriptures to find the truth about this?" They can have a great experience talking with the Lord and reading the Word to discover the truth. They could even ask, "Lord, I thought I heard You say this, but I'm not sure it's right. Is this true, or am I missing something here? I want to hear You and only You speak to me."

Dr. Mark Virkler, who authored 4 *Keys to Hearing God's Voice*, lists five ways we can use to make sure what we are hearing is from God:

1. Test the origin (1 John 4:1).

2. Compare it to biblical principles.

3. Compare it to the names and character of God as revealed in the Bible.

4. Test the fruit (Matthew 7:15-20).

5. Share it with your spiritual counselors (Proverbs 11:14).[6]

To learn more about how to hear God's voice, refer to the article "How to Hear God's Voice" by Dr. Virkler in Appendix A.

Whether you are engaging in PAL for yourself or facilitating ministry with someone else, be diligent in practicing and teaching these principles. Many people are not deeply rooted in the Scriptures and might try living life based on thoughts they think are from God but are not. This has caused confusion and disillusionment for many. A sad ending for some is a state of delusion. Please test what you are hearing using Dr. Virkler's guidelines.

For relationships to deepen in intimacy, questions need to be part of our repertoire. Rather than making assumptions about circumstances or people, we can learn to ask questions for clarification. As we have conversations with people, we often make up a story in our heads about the situation and the people involved. Is the story true, or is it contaminated by our filters of unhealed hurts and wounds? We tend to assign motives to someone's character and begin to think thoughts that affect how we behave toward them. We must learn to ask them if our assumptions are what they want us to think, or we risk misjudging them and basing our relationship with them on those faulty assumptions. When we ask questions to clarify our false narratives, we open the door for genuine intimacy with God and others.

I've raised several questions in this chapter that I will be addressing throughout this book. We will grow in Christlikeness only through conscious, intentional effort as we are taught and led by the Holy Spirit.

Let's begin this journey together and learn about asking questions.

Do you enjoy hearing stories of how God is working in other people's lives? The witness of God's faithfulness for others stirs hope and strengthens our faith to believe He will help us, too. Some of my ministry teammates have graciously shared stories of how questions have influenced their lives in an impactful manner. You will be encouraged as you read them throughout *Life-Changing Questions.*

Enjoy and receive a blessing with each story you read.

# Janet's Story

For some time the idea that I needed to "correctly" express my questions to the Lord frustrated me. So I decided to journal:

Lord, sometimes the idea that I must think of the right way to ask You a question seems daunting or even preposterous. You know everything. Surely You'll understand where I'm coming from. You'll know what I mean. What's the big deal with needing to figure out the exact words to ask? Am I even asking these questions the right way??

*My dear child, I know your questions long before they ever form in your mind or arise from your heart. I also know the answers I long to share with you. My desire is that you think through what you need answers for and lay down your expectations so that your mind and heart are open to hear My voice rather than what you want to hear. I long for My Spirit to have room to increase within you so that our fellowship may be richer and deeper. I rejoice that My rivers of living water are increasingly flowing within you and from you.*

*So ask away. Continue asking and seeking, and I will guide your thoughts and words. I will help you form the right kinds of questions — redemptive questions. And I will love pouring out My answers of understanding, hope, and healing — answers that will "...be a lamp to your feet and a light for your path." I love you, I love you, I love you. You need never question that!*

Janet Willig

# CHAPTER TWO:

## *Why Are Questions So Powerful?*

I HIGHLY APPRECIATE A QUESTION-CENTERED ministry as opposed to being directive-based. At times the directive approach is just what the person needs, but using questions helps people mature in their ability to think through challenging situations and arrive at satisfying and fruitful solutions. Questions have a way of getting us to the heart of the matter causing concern.

People grow in soul transformation by leaps and bounds when they learn how much they can accomplish as they begin to ask questions instead of depending on other people to tell them how to think and what to do. As we ask the Lord questions, people develop increasing confidence in who Jesus is for them as they embrace and apply the wisdom He speaks.

Asking questions requires people to participate in their healing. Jesus modeled asking questions in many ways throughout the Gospels. In chapter three, we will look at the types of questions He asked and how He used them to bring healing and understanding. In this chapter, we'll consider different types of questions and their purposes.

# WRONG ASSUMPTIONS EMPOWER UNREALISTIC EXPECTATIONS!

***Questions can be used as a preventive measure against our tendency to be judgmental.***

When we don't know the answer to something, rather than assume, make up a story in our heads, or assign a motive to someone's character, we learn to ask! We take responsibility for our own thoughts and feelings when we ask so we don't erroneously assume the intent of the person's thought, feeling or behavior. *Wrong assumptions empower unrealistic expectations!* They can lead a whole conversation and state of a relationship off course. We can preface a question with something such as, "I have been thinking this about _____. When I think this way, I feel _____ and then usually act like _____. That isn't what I want. I want to be sure I understand you correctly. I may be totally off base with my thought, and I want to check with you. Is this what you meant/want me to think?" "What was your intention when you said or did _____? or What message were you trying to send to me?" These are alternative ways of asking the same question. We connect with different people depending on how we ask the question.

***Question-centered ministry can be powerful with the understanding that questions are directed to God so we can hear His wisdom.***

Listening to His responses to questions can give us insight for the direction of follow-up questions. The goal is getting to the root issue while keeping the focus of the dialogue with Jesus. God is the source of the wisdom we need (Proverbs 2:6, Daniel 2:20, Colossians 2:3, James 1:5).

*Questions asked of the Lord lead to a more profound knowledge of His character and develop in us an unshakable confidence in our relationship with Him.*

When we have a dialogue with Him, we learn more about His nature and character, how He wants to relate to us, connect with us, teach us, lead us, and guide us. He becomes more than just a word to us, and the dynamic of a life-changing relationship develops as it becomes a 24/7 reality. This dynamic increasingly empowers us to live as citizens of the Kingdom of God rather than default to the kingdom of darkness from which He has delivered us (Colossians 1:13).

Sometimes it is hard to ask the Lord a question because we are afraid of what He might say. We often think, "What if He tells me something I don't want to hear? What if He asks me to do something I'm afraid to do?" I have felt that way myself, but in the deepest place of my heart, I seek His truth because I know that it will lead me to that deeper knowledge and intimacy. His answer will instruct me on how to walk in the power of the Holy Spirit.

We simply need to be honest and say out loud, "Lord, I'm afraid to hear Your answer because I think _____. But I am desperate for something that will help me, so I'm going to step out and ask You anyway." Saying our thoughts out loud has a way of encouraging us. It also puts our soul on notice that we are taking charge and not allowing our emotions to dictate our behavior.

## LORD, WHO ARE YOU RIGHT NOW FOR ME?

### *Questions evoke dialogue.*

Dialogue enhances relationships. Dialoguing is an opportunity for iron to sharpen iron, as the writer of Proverbs 27:17 noted. We seek the results that a dialogue with the most important Person in the universe can produce. We all have questions about life. We can chat with each other and gain some wisdom, but why wouldn't we want to ask the One who *is* wisdom? A dialogue evoking question to ask is, "Lord, who are You right now for me?" He has so many facets to His nature and character that we will spend eternity getting to know Him.

## "NEVER LOSE A HOLY CURIOSITY."
### Albert Einstein

### *Questions can reveal a teachable spirit*

Albert Einstein, known for his creativity and discoveries, is quoted as saying, "The important thing is not to stop questioning." This is the first part of a more extended quote, which ends with the beautiful line: "Never lose a holy curiosity."[7] Just imagine the discoveries we will make about our own journey as we continue to ask questions of the Lord. We will gain wisdom and understanding for the steps He wants us to take when we are wrestling with challenges. He is the Source of all wisdom and the Author of holy curiosity and imagination.

A teachable spirit is necessary for the process of transformation. Change is an inevitable element in transformation. If we think we have all the answers already, we won't be flexible enough to welcome and receive what God desires to bring to maturity. Questions help us develop a holy curiosity that opens doors to creative solutions God can use to move us forward on our journey into wholeness. Humility positions us to rise; pride positions us to fail and fall. Humility allows the heart to PAL: "I am willing to consider I could be wrong. I will inquire of the Lord to search my heart. Lord, is there something You want to show me in my heart right now about this issue?" Be sure to take time to listen!

## LORD, IS THERE ANOTHER WAY FOR ME TO THINK ABOUT THIS PERSON OR SITUATION?

Questions can have the power to change an attitude of "I'm right – you need to think like I think," to "I'm willing to entertain another perspective." A good question to ask to discern if an attitude or thought needs to be changed is, "Lord, is there another way for me to think about this person or situation? I want to walk in freedom, so would You let me know what You think about this?"

### *Questions invite people to take responsibility for their own lives.*

We must remember that no friend, pastor, or counselor is the answer to another person's need. They cannot fix anyone else's problem. They are not anyone's power source. Each of us must participate in our own healing journey. Rather than asking for another and hearing for them, how much more productive would it be for the person's growth if they learn how to ask good questions, hear the answers, and how to put them into practice? This presents an opportunity to develop wisdom.

Many of us don't know how to apply the truth of the Word to daily life. We can know the Word of God, but stumble when we try to put His truth into practice. Part of asking questions is pressing in with more questions: "What does this mean for me right now in my life? How can I practice this truth? How will my behavior look different if I receive and embrace this truth?"

### *Questions lead to reflection that results in peace*
### *when we hear, embrace and obey the voice of the Lord.*

When we are struggling and confused about something, most likely we are not experiencing peace. When we are *in* Christ, we experience peace, because He *is* Peace. Hearing His voice speak to us reminds us of this truth. He is a God who loves to talk with His children and show us how He wants to live His life through us all the time. He wants to express His nature and character to each of us and, through us, to the world. The great exchange is that He has offered and continues to offer us the truth of Galatians 2:20: "I have been crucified with Christ; and it is no longer I who live, but Christ lives *in* me; and the life which I now live in the flesh I live by faith in the Son of God, who loved me and gave Himself up for me." This exchanged life is a reality in the Kingdom of God. It is a life-long journey of learning to "let go and let God."

### *Questions lead to dependence on the Holy Spirit for wisdom and truth rather than our own reasoning powers.*

If a person takes a considerable amount of time waiting for an answer and they seem to be struggling, they have quite likely moved from a place of listening in their spirit to trying to figure it out for themselves. When this happens, it helps them to pause for a moment, refocus, and begin again to listen for the Lord's answer. An effective question to facilitate this is, "Are you struggling to figure out an answer, or are you still in a quiet place listening for God?" This insight is crucial because when the person does eventually hear something, it is far beyond what they could think up on their own. Wisdom from Heaven is what we all need – it is worth pressing into and waiting for. PAL – Pause, Ask, Listen – is highly effective in obtaining the wisdom and revelation available when we ask (James 1:5).

### *Questions help convert a worldly, problem-oriented focus to a Godly, solution-oriented focus.*

Much of our society and culture concentrates on what is wrong. What is wrong with me? With you? We look to place blame elsewhere, spending an enormous amount of energy on issues that result in a negative outcome. But the Holy Spirit will always lead us to His solution when we ask Him. Wouldn't it be more productive to use our energy to ask solution-oriented questions? What if we learn to change our questions from "What's wrong with me?" to "Lord, who do You want to be in/for/through me right now? What do You want me to see and understand in order for me to walk in peace and freedom?" What if we ask questions like "What do You want me to learn during my season in this job? What are You teaching me?" instead of "Why am I in this dead-end job? Why are all these people against me? Why are they so stupid?"

## WHAT THOUGHTS ARE PRODUCING THESE BEHAVIORS IN MY LIFE?

*Questions empower paradigm changes.*

Questions enable us to get in touch with how we view God, others, ourselves, and our circumstances. When the fruit in our life is ungodly, it is time to ask the vital question: "Lord, things aren't going well for me now, so I must be thinking something that isn't good for me. What thoughts are producing these behaviors in my life?" A change of perspective is needed when we are looking for a new behavior. *What we believe determines how we behave.*

Martin Copenhaver, retired president of Andover Newton Theological School, states it this way: "By entertaining questions God has a chance to change us. Answers can be offered as a conclusion. Questions are an invitation to further reflection. For the most part, answers close and questions open".[8] There is always more to explore when God is part of the equation. Ask Him, and the doors of possibilities keep opening.

## WHAT WE BELIEVE DETERMINES HOW WE BEHAVE.

### *Questions can alter the course of our lives.*

Questions inspired by the Holy Spirit enable us to change the course of our lives. Most of our inner dialogues are question-based and reflect habit patterns arising from our nature before becoming a new creation. Habit patterns of thought formed before being made "new" empower the nature of the "old man" to feel and behave according to those old patterns. We are controlled by a set of rules and regulations that set us up with an overwhelming need to perform – and we usually fail. The Apostle Paul gives clear instructions to "put off the old man" and "put on the new man" as he describes how we are to walk in the power of the Spirit (Romans 6:6; Galatians 3:27, 5:16-18, 25; Ephesians 4:22-24, 5:3; Colossians 3:5-10). He also instructs us to "be transformed by renewing our minds" (Romans 12:2). That means the way we think radically changes how we feel and behave as we become more like Jesus.

As previously mentioned, our inner dialogue is usually negative and takes us in a shaming, self-condemning direction. Asking questions has the power to open doors to Holy Spirit-led discoveries of adventure and fulfillment we never thought existed until we asked. Ephesians 3:20 says, "God is able, through His mighty power at work in us, to accomplish more than we might ask or think." What would happen if we decided to ask, and ask big? It might be appropriate to PAL, "I'm stuck here right now. I'm frustrated about how life is going for me. It's not what I want or thought I would have. Would You help me? What do You want me to see, hear and know right now?" We can either open the door to the future by asking risky questions to which we do not know the answers or decide to never open the door. Following the Holy Spirit involves taking risks. Fear keeps us from asking and obeying – but fear is not an option in the Kingdom of God – only perfect love.

## FEAR IS NOT AN OPTION IN THE KINGDOM OF GOD – ONLY PERFECT LOVE.

## Types of Questions

Different types of questions meet different needs. Following is a list of some of those types of questions:

*Closed/Open Ended*

Closed questions can usually be answered with one word. There is no invitation to an ongoing dialogue, and therefore no opportunity to develop the relationship.

> For example: Closed: Can you _____? How was your day? Did you have any challenges today? Do you know what that looks like or means?

Open-ended questions invite details in the information shared.

> For example: Open-ended: How can you _____? What was the best part about your day? The most challenging? What does that mean/look like to you?

*Discovery*

> "Lord Jesus, what do You want for me in this situation?"

> "Jesus, what do you want me to learn?"

> "Jesus, what are some of the judgments I have made about people/situations that led me to this point?"

> "Jesus, is there anyone you want me to forgive so I can walk in freedom?"

> "Jesus, what consequences am I living with today as a result of the words or actions of this person?"

> "Jesus, is there another way for me to think about this situation so I can agree with You?"

*Condemning/Judging*

> Why am I always doing this wrong?
>
> Why am I so stupid?
>
> Why can't I ever get this right?
>
> Why is this person so controlling? Judgmental? Domineering? Confused? (Put your own words here.)
>
> Why try?
>
> Why bother anymore?

"Why" questions are usually argumentative and put people on the defensive. They tend to take the focus off of the real issue and cause the person to use their energy to defend their behavior.

*Focusing*

> "Lord, I seem to be all over the map and not able to focus right now. Would You help me? What issue in my life (thought, emotion out of balance, behavior) do You want to talk to me about today? What thought, feeling or behavior is hindering my journey?"

Focusing questions help us think about and deal with one issue at a time. Otherwise, we become confused and overwhelmed. Focusing on one problem at a time clears the mind of clutter, strengthening the ability to think clearly.

*Refocusing*

> "Lord, will You help me ask a question that enables me to see Your possibilities instead of what's wrong with myself or others?" A refocusing question might be, "How would You like for me to think about this?" Or, "Is there another way for me to think about this?" Refocusing questions help us discern better ways to think and choose a Kingdom of God perspective versus a kingdom of darkness perspective.

We will explore discovery, condemning/judging, focusing, and refocusing questions in chapters five through seven. Recognizing the differences in these questions is a primary key to help facilitate the transformation in a believer's life.

## Teaching

With teaching questions, the answer is embedded in the question itself. We could ask, "Do you think this sin you have committed is too big for God to forgive?" Instead, let's PAL, "Lord, is this sin too big for You to forgive?" These two questions imply the answer (which is "No"), but the second one allows the person to interact with the Lord and hear Him speak a fresh word to their heart. The person will experience hearing the truth of God's word and realizing that nothing is too big for God to forgive. They can know the truth in their mind *and* experience it in their heart as they hear and receive.

This type of question is an effective tool to keep the person's focus on engaging with the Lord instead of having a dialogue with you.

## Encouraging

Perhaps a person has chosen their way instead of God's and feels foolish and condemned. A direct statement such as, "Well, you know God's way is always the best way," reinforces these feelings. Asking encouraging questions empowers that person to think about their choices and releases them to choose God's way. Some examples might be, "Could you share a time when you experienced knowing that God's way is always the best way for you? How might knowing that help you in this situation?"

Consider this PAL: "Lord, I have made some choices that have resulted in my current situation. Would You please forgive me? What can I choose now that will lead me on a better path?"

Many different types of questions facilitate connecting people with Jesus. A great question to determine what to ask in a given situation might be, "Lord, what does this person need right now? What can they ask You to help them progress in the freedom You have given them?"

Let's journey on and look at how Jesus used questions.

# Mike's Story

When I was in my early twenties, I realized I needed help in dealing with some of my struggles. I decided to utilize a healing ministry that our church offered. Getting started required me to fill out a questionnaire regarding the issue that I was seeking help overcoming. The questionnaire, as you can imagine, was full of questions designed to help me share background and the focus for which I wanted help. I filled in the answers to all the questions as best I could, anticipating that God was going to do something incredible through this ministry.

I was feeling pretty good about the direction I thought that I needed to go. Then came the very last question. It read something to the effect of, "Now ask the Holy Spirit if there is anything else He would like to speak to me about regarding my issue." Have you ever heard the saying, "Your problem isn't really your problem, but rather a symptom of a greater problem"? I had filled out my questionnaire thinking I knew what my problem was, but in reality I was only skimming the surface.

In due diligence I sought to ask the Holy Spirit if there was anything else He wanted to add. He began to bring to mind a memory from the not-so-distant past. I had just arrived home from a seven-month mission trip to Mexico. I was exhausted physically, emotionally, and spiritually. Coming home was all I wanted to do, and I had anticipated what my "welcome home" was going to be like. I remember walking in the house and instantly smelling my mom's cooking. I figured she was fixing up a huge meal, perhaps some of my favorite foods, and having the whole family home to welcome me back. I walked into the kitchen and saw my mom standing at the stove. I walked up next to her, put my arm around her, and asked what she was making. She said that she and my dad were having friends over and I could stay if I wanted. To be honest I was shocked, but I didn't know what to say. I just stuffed my emotions and acted like everything was okay.

I began to write down what the Holy Spirit was showing me. Every time I tried to write, I became overwhelmed with the hurt that I had buried and began to sob to the point I couldn't see. I would get myself back to being able to see and write, but as soon as I started, I began sobbing again. This went on for almost twenty minutes. I realized I was never going to be able to finish until I let it all out. I locked myself into a room and just cried it all out until I had nothing left in me. The memory that I had buried like so many others became a key to experiencing freedom, healing, and the Father-heart of God for me.

Asking the Holy Spirit what He wanted to show or say to me rather than relying on my limited view helped me unlock that memory and many more that I had buried. Now when I struggle, I first try to ask Him, "What do You want to say to me about this issue?"

Mike Fox

# CHAPTER THREE:

## *Jesus Questions*

HAVE YOU EVER SENSED JESUS ASKING YOU A question like, "What do *you* think about this?" or "What do *you* want to do?" in response to your questions to Him? Perhaps you have been seriously wrestling with a job change or a geographic location change for your family. You've been praying, asking, searching, and looking for discernment, and you hear Jesus asking you a question in answer to your question. Seriously?

When our children were sixteen and thirteen, we were considering a move from the Houston, Texas, area to northern Indiana. It was a very difficult process to work through the decision. Not only were our children at vulnerable ages for such a major change, we would be going in the middle of winter from a warm, humid climate to freezing cold snow and ice country. We were not happy about that and certainly not prepared with our wardrobes! We wanted to at least wait until summertime when the children would be out of school and the weather would be more inviting. But we were sensing in our spirits God saying, "GO NOW!" Our hearts struggled. Finally, one day as I was spouting off all the cons of moving in the middle of winter and what to do about schooling for the children, I heard the Lord say, "What do *you* want, Carolyn?" I got really quiet. You know when the Lord asks you a question, it's probably time to settle down, think, and listen.

Finally I said, "Lord, at the depth of my being I want only what You want for my family and me. I know whatever that is will be best for us." I realized I had been trying to weigh all the possibilities and rehearse the bad things that could happen, so I was missing the peace available to step into His leading and start moving.

It took a question from Jesus to arrest the striving, fears, doubts, and resistance long enough to hear clearly. A conversation with Jesus about a lot of those fears was necessary. I also needed to surrender my desires and accept His. The excuses for waiting or not going at all began to fade as God dealt with my heart. And it all started with His arresting question, "What do *you* want, Carolyn?"

Jesus is our example when it comes to living life in the Kingdom of God. We can learn so much from Him about asking questions. How I wish we could hear the tone of voice Jesus used as he taught the disciples and the crowds! We depend so much on verbal cues and body language to interpret meaning. Is someone upset, or gentle and inquiring? Even when Jesus wanted to get a challenging point across to His hearers, He didn't want the result to be shame and condemnation, but rather a realization of wrong thinking and behavior that, when recognized, could lead to redemption.

## JESUS USED QUESTIONS IN SEVERAL DIFFERENT WAYS AS HE INTERACTED WITH PEOPLE.

Jesus used questions in several different ways as He interacted with people. In the Gospel accounts, He asked several hundred questions. Although we can't look at all of the accounts, I've selected a few to see what principles we can glean from His example.

### Reality Check Questions

One of my favorite questions is in John 5 when Jesus asked a lame man if he wanted to get well. The man responded that he had no one to put him in the healing waters when they were stirred. Others would get to the pool before him because of his condition, and only the first one in would be healed. Ignoring this reality and the rule against working on the Sabbath, Jesus commanded him to get up, pick up his pallet, and walk. Jesus told the man to carry his pallet on the Sabbath, He healed on the Sabbath, and then claimed that God was His Father. What was He thinking?? Three strikes! We would have put Jesus out of the game for making this many errors.

The good news is the lame man obeyed and was healed immediately. What work was Jesus doing in this man's heart by asking this curious question: "Do you want to get well?" Was He testing the man's level of desperation? Was He discerning his heart? Was He putting the audience on notice that something was about to happen? What was the fruit of this question? A healing? A witness to the community? A testimony about Who Jesus is and Who His Father is? A confrontation with the Pharisees with an opportunity for them to see the truth? These are some of the results that followed His question. Jesus started a conversation with a question that affected many people beyond the man to whom the question was directed.

### Challenging and Confrontational Questions

The questions Jesus asked were sometimes challenging and confrontational. "Did you never read in the Scriptures…" He asked of the Pharisees in Matthew 21:42, confronting their hypocrisy. After all, weren't they the experts in knowing and keeping the letter of the law? Who should have the audacity to question or disagree with them? These types of questions force the hearers to be honest with themselves.

### Search the Heart Questions

Sometimes the questions compelled the hearer to think deeply and search their heart for an answer that called for a response of change. Such was the question Jesus posed in Matthew 16:26: "What profit would there be for one to gain the whole world and forfeit his life, and what can one give in exchange for his life?" Questions like this tend to pull us out of our comfort zone and life as usual. They cause us to re-evaluate our choices about how we spend our time, energy, partnerships, and money. "Am I doing what Jesus wants me to be doing with my life? Am I making Godly choices?"

### *Looking for Information, Making a Point Questions*

Jesus asked questions to get an informational response. Then He would make a point. An example of this is demonstrated in Mark 8:1-10. The crowds had been gathered for several days listening to Jesus, and they didn't have anything to eat. He didn't want to send them away hungry. The disciples asked Him, "Where would we get so many loaves in this desolate place to satisfy such a large crowd?"

Jesus responded by asking, "How many loaves do you have?" He was making a point that He could perform miracles when they gave Him whatever they had, even if it was only seven loaves and a few small fish. In the same way, He will perform miracles for us when we give Him what we have, no matter how small or seemingly insignificant. When the disciples collected the leftovers after the crowds had eaten, they had seven full baskets. I think Jesus used this method of asking a question to make them aware of the situation and help them get in touch with His nature of being a miracle worker. He was teaching them about faith and learning how to offer to Him challenging situations to see what He would do, or what He could do *through them* to achieve resolution.

### *Rhetorical Questions*

Jesus used rhetorical questions, sometimes several in a row, to get across a point and communicate His passion and intensity about a situation or subject. Shortly after feeding the crowds with multiplied loaves and fish, Jesus found himself in a boat with the disciples. He was fresh off an encounter with the Pharisees, who wanted to argue with Him and test Him. The disciples had forgotten to take bread with them and had only one loaf. Jesus started warning them about the leaven of the Pharisees and Herod.

The disciples didn't get the point of the conversation and started talking about the fact they had no bread. Aware of this, Jesus said to them, "Why do you discuss the fact you have no bread? Do you have a hardened heart? Having eyes, do you not see? Having ears, do you not hear? Do you not remember when I broke the five loaves for the five thousand, how many baskets full of broken pieces you picked up? (Mark 6:38) When I broke the seven for the four thousand, how many large baskets full of broken pieces did you pick up? Do you not yet understand?" (Mark 8:14-21)

He could have said, "Guys c'mon! Really!" But by asking these questions he was making His point: when I am involved, you don't need to worry about things like what you are going to eat. Pay attention to the things that can harm you – like what the Pharisees and the system they stand for can do when you partake of them.

### *Correcting Questions*

Some Pharisees and scribes from Jerusalem asked Jesus why his disciples were breaking the tradition of the elders by not washing their hands when they ate bread. Jesus replied with a question that pointed out their hypocrisy: "Why do you yourselves transgress the commandment of God for the sake of your tradition? For God said, 'Honor your father and mother,' and, 'He who speaks evil of his father or mother is to be put to death.' But you say, 'Whoever says to his father or mother "Whatever I have that would help you has been given to God,"' he is not to honor his father or mother.' And by this you invalidated the word of God for the sake of your tradition. You hypocrites, rightly did Isaiah prophesy of you: This people honors Me with their lips, but their heart is far away from Me. But in vain do they worship Me, teaching as doctrines the precepts of men'" (Matthew 15:1-9).

Then Jesus pointed this out to the crowd that was present: "Hear and understand. It is not what enters into the mouth that defiles the man, but what proceeds out of the mouth, this defiles the man" (Matthew 15:10-11).

The disciples asked Jesus, "Do You know that the Pharisees were offended when they heard this statement?" Jesus replied, "Every plant which My heavenly Father did not plant shall be uprooted. Let them alone; they are blind guides of the blind. And if a blind man guides a blind man, both will fall into a pit" (Matthew 15:13-14).

The Pharisees, the crowd, and the disciples all heard something important from Jesus that day in response to the question He asked: "Why do you yourselves transgress the commandment of God for the sake of your tradition?" (Matthew 15:2)

Questions can arrest the hearer, causing them to stop, think, and be ready for what will be said next.

### Seeking Feedback Questions

Jesus and the disciples were in Bethsaida after the feeding of the four thousand. The crowd brought a blind man to Jesus and begged Him to touch and heal him. Jesus took him by the hand, led him out of the village, spit on his eyes, placed His hands on the man's eyes, and asked, "Do you see anything?" At first the man saw men that looked like trees walking around. When Jesus laid hands on the man's eyes again, his sight was fully restored (Mark 8:22-26).

Why Jesus even asked a question and then needed to touch the man's eyes twice is a mystery. He could have spoken a word and the healing would have happened. But Jesus modeled for us an important practice to use when we pray for people. We need to know what is going on, and asking a question is the best way to get the feedback we need to move ahead in our healing journey. This story also encourages us to keep pressing in for results and not give up after one try or one encounter. Sometimes healing is a process.

## SOMETIMES HEALING IS A PROCESS.

Some great questions that allow for helpful feedback are, "Is what I'm saying connecting with you? Is this making sense to you? Can you tell me what you are hearing me say? Can you tell me what is happening for you right now?"

### *Making a Statement Questions*

It had been reported that the synagogue official's daughter had died, so he didn't need to ask Jesus to come pray for her healing. But Jesus had the final word in this situation. He told the official, "Do not be afraid any longer, only believe." When Jesus arrived at the house where the daughter lay, there was a big commotion with weeping and wailing. When he entered, His question to the people was, "Why make a commotion and weep? The child has not died but is asleep." They laughed and made fun of Him, but that didn't stop Jesus from being persistent, praying for the girl, and raising her from the dead (Mark 5:35-43).

With His question, Jesus seemed to be making the statement, "Stop this behavior that is based on your emotions. I'm here now. There is no need for this. It is time to have faith in Me."

By asking a question, Jesus caused the people to stop. He gave them an opportunity to rethink their position. Would they choose to believe in what they saw with their physical eyes – or in this Person, Jesus, who was traveling around the country performing miracles?

### *Invitational Questions*

I love invitational questions, especially ones asked by Jesus. He asked blind Bartimaeus a question for which He surely knew the answer. "What do you want Me to do for you?" You can read the complete, exciting account in Mark 10:46-52. Bartimaeus was being loud and crying out for Jesus to do something for him. People were trying to quiet him down. But his persistence stirred a responsive chord in Jesus' heart that caused Him to reach out with His invitation.

Sometimes we think we know what someone wants based on what we see or know about them. That is not always an accurate guideline. It is good to ask, "What would you like Jesus to do for you today?" Another way to ask this question is, "What is Jesus doing today and how can you participate with Him?"

Jesus had a unique way of using the questions He asked to invite people into a conversation with Him. His goal was an invitation to participate with Him in Kingdom life and work. He didn't always need to impart information.

As He did in the Gospel narrative, He continues to place a high value on partnership with us and often uses questions to provoke us to respond with a hearty "Yes" to His invitations.

Jesus used questions like the ones I've chosen for this chapter to illustrate that there was always fruit produced as a result of the questions. His questions invite us to think. They often require a deep look into our hearts. We can pray along with the Psalmist David, "Search me, O God, and know my heart; Try me and know my anxious thoughts, and see if there be any hurtful way in me and lead me in the everlasting way" (Psalm 139:23-24).

Ungodly motivations and thoughts are revealed as we ponder the questions Jesus asks. We might even hear the Holy Spirit ask a timely question that will soften our hearts and lead us on our way to walk in freedom with the Holy Spirit.

## PAL: PAUSE, ASK, LISTEN

What is your favorite story in the Gospels about Jesus? Did He ask any questions that arrest your attention? As I mentioned, there are several hundred questions that deserve our consideration. Appendix B of this book lists some PAL (Pause, Ask, Listen) activations centered on some of the questions Jesus asked in the Gospels. They are designed for you to use as devotionals to facilitate quality time spent dialoguing with the Lord. What implications might you glean for practical application in your own life? Some general questions to PAL when you read one of these activations are:

- What opportunity does this question give me to embrace a truth?

- How does this apply to me in my life right now?

- Lord Jesus, would You cause the truth of what You were saying (to the disciples, the Pharisees, etc.) to penetrate my heart so I can be more like You?

The answers to these questions and others invite us to a better way when we may have been settling for something less. Jesus is always after the "more" of the change that happens when we are transformed by renewing our minds. He modeled for us how to use questions to produce change and growth. Let's do the same.

# Carolyn's Story

Over forty years ago, my Sunday School class was studying the book of Acts. One Sunday the woman sitting next to me leaned over and asked, "Why don't we do this stuff here?" The "stuff" she referred to was praying for the sick and demonized, being filled with the Spirit, and speaking in other tongues.

My first response was indignation because I thought she was putting down our church and the leadership (my husband Ron). I thought, "How dare you impugn my heritage and my church!" I was offended – furious. I can't even remember my verbal response because I was so upset.

I went home that day and sobbed. I cried out to God, "Why don't we do that stuff here? It's in the Bible. Why can't we do it?" For years my religious tradition had taught me that "stuff" wasn't for today; speaking in tongues was of the devil. But I struggled, thinking that couldn't be true. I was hungry for more in my journey with God. I knew there had to be more. I was experiencing a holy dissatisfaction.

But I had heard terrifying stories about people who spoke in tongues. They ran on the back of pews during church, rolled in the aisles, and foamed at the mouth. I was a shy, quiet person. If I had to subject myself to that kind of behavior, I was going to say, "No, thank you" – not only because of my personality but also because of fear of what people would think of me.

I faced a dilemma. I wanted everything God had for me so I could experience the peace I read about in Scripture and so I could exercise the gifts of the Spirit and know Him intimately. I was hungry and thirsty. I had to decide whether to let tradition and fear of man rule my head and heart... or allow God to help me change my beliefs and practices.

I felt as if there was no safe place for me to voice my thoughts and feelings. If I expressed my opinions, I might be labeled as suspect, and a threat to my husband's job could become a reality. What would we do if we lost financial provision for our family? What would become of our reputation in our church tradition? What if my tradition's teachings were in error?

Was I doomed to a dissatisfied life? Was I trapped?

That innocent question, "Why don't we do this stuff here?" led me on a journey of questioning God, tradition, and the Scriptures. What is true? What am I willing to give up or exchange for the truth? What will change in my life if I discover I have believed a lie and it has held me back from knowing and doing what God designed for me?

Being willing to lay down my pride and let God do what He wanted to do was huge for me. Could I trust Him?

My husband and I went through a period of disappointment, discouragement and disillusionment. After many prayers for discernment, we eventually heard the Lord say to us, "Come apart, or come apart."

We chose to follow a path of discovery. The result of saying "Yes" to God began both a painful and exhilarating journey – one I wouldn't trade. My pride was challenged. I needed to submit to Him my fear of losing reputation and position. He was asking for my whole "Yes" so I could experience a deeper relationship with Him.

As it happened, none of the stories I had heard about speaking in tongues and being full of the Holy Spirit happened to me. God was so gentle. I was at home alone in my den when the Lord met me in my desperation. Sitting down to have quiet time with Him, I opened my Bible to the book of John and began to read out loud. I don't know why I did that; I had never read Scripture out loud for devotions. "In the beginning was the Word, and the Word was with God, and..." Suddenly from the depths of my being flowed a warm river of words – words I didn't understand. It was as if a dam had broken inside me and the words were gushing out with a mighty force. I was aware of God's presence being so close – surrounding me.

I felt like dancing and singing and playing like a child – so I did. I was meeting with God, the Creator of the universe – my Creator. The sense of His love for me was overwhelming.

God gave me a wonderful confirmation that this was truly a new prayer language given by Him and not of the devil. When Ron heard me speak in the prayer language, he recognized it as German, since His grandmother had spoken German in the home when he was a child. I was saying things like, "I praise You O most high God, Creator of the universe. Only You are worthy." This was truly a gift from God!

There was no running on the back of pews, no rolling down the aisles and no foaming at the mouth. I felt a freedom I had never felt before in my life. I was not embarrassed in front of my friends or colleagues. God's kindness was tangible.

Although it took some time before I was comfortable exercising this new-found freedom in corporate worship, my journey into the realm of knowing God intimately with freedom in the Spirit had just taken a huge step.

That question asked over forty years ago launched me into a life of stepping out in faith, listening to the Holy Spirit guiding and instructing me to say and do things not possible for someone who doesn't believe "that stuff is for today."

It took just one question to jar me loose so I could ask many other questions that were part of my inner dialogue, but I had been afraid to ask.

Don't be afraid – ask away.

Carolyn Allen

# CHAPTER FOUR:

## *Did God Really Say That?*

*The Lord God placed the man in the Garden of Eden to tend and watch over it. But the Lord God warned him, "You may freely eat the fruit of every tree in the garden - except the tree of the knowledge of good and evil. If you eat its fruit, you are sure to die" (Genesis 2:15-17 NLT).*

*The serpent was the shrewdest of all the wild animals the Lord God had made. One day he asked the woman, "Did God really say you must not eat the fruit from any of the trees in the garden?"*

*"Of course, we may eat fruit from the trees in the garden," the woman replied. "It's only the fruit from the tree in the middle of the garden that we are not allowed to eat. God said, "You must not eat it or even touch it; if you do, you will die."*

*"You won't die!" the serpent replied to the woman. "God knows that your eyes will be opened as soon as you eat it, and you will be like God, knowing both good and evil."*

*The woman was convinced. She saw that the tree was beautiful, and its fruit looked delicious, and she wanted the wisdom it would give her. So she took some of the fruit and ate it. Then she gave some to her husband, who was with her, and he ate it, too. At that moment their eyes were opened, and they suddenly felt shame at their nakedness. So they sewed fig leaves together to cover themselves.*

*When the cool evening breezes were blowing, the man and his wife heard the Lord God walking about in the garden. So they hid from the Lord God among the trees. Then the Lord God called to the man, "Where are you?"*

*He replied, "I heard you walking in the garden, so I hid. I was afraid because I was naked."*

*"Who told you that you were naked?" the Lord God asked. "Have you eaten from the tree whose fruit I commanded you not to eat?"*

*The man replied, "It was the woman you gave me who gave me the fruit, and I ate it."*

*Then the Lord God asked the woman, "What have you done?"*

*"The serpent deceived me," she replied. "That's why I ate it"* *(Genesis 3:1-13 NLT).*

WE HAVE AN ENEMY WHOSE MISSION IS TO STEAL from us, kill us, and destroy us (John 10:10). He knows how to use questions effectively in this endeavor. The Apostle Peter admonishes us to "Stay alert! Watch out for your great enemy, the devil. He prowls around like a roaring lion looking for someone to devour. Stand firm against him and be strong in your faith" (1 Peter 5:8-9a). In order to accomplish this, we need to know the enemy's strategy so that we can recognize when he is the instigator of the dialogue in our minds.

When Satan started that conversation with Eve, he began with a question – a question designed to entice her on a path leading to condemnation, deception and destruction. His question, "Did God really say…" caused Eve to start thinking, "Is this really a sin? Did God really mean that? Why would He say that? Why would He do that to us? He must not want the best for us.

We have a right to know what He knows. We shouldn't let ourselves be taken advantage of. Really, we can be like God. We should go for it. We deserve it."

Eve's progression to destruction started with some truth included. But the enemy's driving intention when he asked, "Did God really say…?" was to stir doubt in the character and motivations of God so Eve wouldn't trust Him. This sowed a seed of doubt, which she accepted and began to apply to her decision-making. He also poked at Eve's desire to use her intellectual abilities to know and be like God. As a result, she started down the path to deception, which led to disobedience and eventually death and separation from God.

## IS THIS QUESTION LEADING ME TO DOUBT THE CHARACTER AND NATURE OF GOD?

In our own lives, we must learn to ask ourselves, "Is this question leading me to doubt the character and nature of God? Is it causing me to judge someone in a negative way? Is it resulting in self-condemnation and shaming?" As we begin to recognize this, we are on track to discern the source of the question and resulting thoughts. We learn to reject and renounce (disown) any of these kinds of thoughts as soon as possible; this will guard against building harmful strongholds that will later need to be demolished. The longer we hold ungodly perspectives, the more entrenched those ways of thinking become. In the future, it becomes a challenge to tear down ungodly thought patterns and replace them with Godly thoughts. We must learn to discern what we accept as truth by asking good questions.

We can see the same idea in James 1: "…ask in faith without any doubting, for the one who doubts is like the surf of the sea, driven and tossed by the wind. For that man ought not to expect that he will receive anything from the Lord, being a double-minded man, unstable in all his ways. Each one is tempted when he is carried away and enticed by his own lust. Then when lust has conceived, it gives birth to sin; and when sin is accomplished, it brings forth death" (James 1:6-7, 14-15).

## WE HAVE THE POWER TO CHOOSE WHAT PATH TO TAKE, AND IT CAN BEGIN WITH ASKING QUESTIONS.

Doubt – Drawn away by desire – Deception – Disobedience – Death. Not a very inviting path, is it? The telling point is where the path ends, and the fruit of the choice to listen to the accusations and doubts is always death. The wonderful truth is that we have the power to choose what path to take, and it can begin with asking questions that will lead us along the path of discovery with the Holy Spirit. We will explore this concept in future chapters. We need to be aware, though, that some of our questions can be sourced from and used by the enemy. He is known as the "accuser of the brethren," so be on the lookout for questions and thoughts that accuse and condemn. The target of the accusations and condemnation can be God, others and/or self (Revelation 12:10).

## HOW DID I COME TO THAT CONCLUSION?

Discerning the source of the questions and thoughts we entertain is crucial to what path we will choose to take – a path of discovery or a path of condemnation, shame and judgment. The latter leads to death instead of the life God always desires and provides for us. Asking the question, "Who told me that?" helps me realize I might be listening to a source that does not have my best interest at heart. Another good question is, "How did I come to that conclusion?" Or, "Lord, what do You want to say to me about this?"

As followers of Jesus Christ we are blessed to have the Holy Spirit as a constant presence to lead us on our path of transformation. God is continually working through His Holy Spirit to change us to look like His Son Jesus Christ (2 Corinthians 3:18). Rather than setting our own goals for our lives, we are empowered by God to discover them. Revelation from God releases an energy for life that is unequaled by human ingenuity.

Discovery is exciting, especially when led by the Creator of the Universe. Is there anyone more creative than our Creator? Questions play an important role in this discovery process. As I have mentioned before in this book, we ask ourselves questions in our inner dialogue throughout our day. We can learn to ask these questions from a discovery-based perspective rather than through a negative lens to focus on possible solutions instead of the problem.

Condemning questions are law-based, personality-focused and problem-oriented. Discovery questions are love-based, issue-focused and solution-oriented.

Let's determine to ask questions that produce life instead of death. Ready?

# Dakota's Story

One day as I was driving, I realized I was angry about a lot of situations. So I began to pour out my frustrations to God. I wasn't mad at Him; I was just venting the anger stored up inside me to Him. So many things were distressing me: the world, the systems, with people in power, the loss of life, and myriad injustices all around me. I was condemning many people and felt myself spiraling out of control when I told God that an eternity in hell wasn't enough punishment for people responsible for causing evil in the world.

When I took a breath from my ranting, I sensed God asking *me* two questions. He first asked, "What do you know about hell?" I had just been studying about heaven and hell, so I started rehearsing what I'd learned. I talked about the horrors, punishment and torment described in the Scripture. God patiently listened as I spoke about the details of the darkness and depravity of hell.

Then He asked me His second question, "What do you know about time?" I told Him about my concept of time being endless lists of numbers that stretch on and on to the point of incomprehension.

When I finished, God allowed me to experience a glimpse of hell that has forever changed the way I view the forces of good and evil, heaven and hell, and sin and judgment. During my brief journey, I saw and felt total depravity, darkness and terror. The short time that this lasted felt like an eternity. The pain, fear, and dread were too much to bear.

God also allowed me to experience His mercy and grace, which has impacted my understanding of His compassion, sovereignty, and love. For example, in response to my statement that "An eternity in hell isn't enough punishment for people responsible for causing evil in the world," He said, "The longer a person spends in hell, the worse it becomes." Ouch. I hadn't thought about that concept of time as it related to hell.

However, His mercy and grace began to flood my soul when He lovingly whispered, "But Dakota, the longer you spend with Me in heaven, the better and better things get."

The journey with Jesus that day included experiences of both punishment and pleasure. While God was open to my curiosity, He wanted to show me His wisdom as He unraveled His mysteries. My questions and judgments about what people deserve led to an experience that has changed how I approach questioning God and appeasing my curious nature.

I realized anew that God is God. I am not. He knows the bigger picture and has put Kingdom principles in place to empower me to live His way. His ways are higher than mine, and his thoughts are higher than mine (Isaiah 55:8).

What began with a bad attitude led to regret and repentance for how I presented my questions to God. I had been accusing Him and acting as if I knew more than He did.

I have learned that while my questions can be full of life and curiosity, they can also lead me down a dangerous road. I am learning to check my attitude and motivations as I press forward in my curiosity. I can ask myself, "What is going on in my heart? What is the best way to find out what I need to know to move forward?" These principles are valid not only when asking questions to God, but also to other people.

I am also more aware that I'm usually not ready for the answers God will give me, simply because He thinks on a different plane than I do. And that's okay – He's God, and I'm not.

Dakota Brooks

# CHAPTER FIVE:

## Condemning Questions

IN MY BOOK *Journey into Wholeness* I SHARED ABOUT the moment I realized that I was living some areas of my life from the mindset of a victim. I share it again here because that realization led to the beginning of recognizing self-condemning, shaming questions.

> *Sometimes we have blind spots, wrong beliefs that keep us from discerning lies we believe and cause us to feel and act in ungodly ways. If we keep getting results we don't like, we might suspect that we have a blind spot and realize that we need to do something to change, and sometimes we need each other's help to see these blind spots.*

> *I discovered I had one of those blind spots with the help of a counselor friend. He stayed in our home when he visited to minister at Heartland Church, so he had ample opportunity to observe our home life. He is gifted in counsel and wisdom, and when he observed certain interchanges between Ron and me, he could see and feel beyond the spoken. Can anyone relate?*

> *Our friend observed one of these interchanges between Ron and me. We had invited him into our lives on a level of vulnerability and accountability. We knew we needed a peer to speak truth*

*into our lives. We wanted to grow and change, so when he came to our home, we usually set aside time for each of us to talk for counsel. These conversations usually led to some "robust" dialogue!*

*I don't even remember the issue that prompted a conversation with me, but he noticed I was angry about something Ron said and did. Although I stuffed it, I carried around an attitude about it. He wanted to know where the emotion was coming from.*

*Something like this came out of my mouth, "I was angry because I thought if Ron would only change his behavior and tone of voice, then I could be something different myself. I could do and be all that God wants me to be." Wow. I said it. The earth didn't tremble, and I wasn't struck dead.*

*Almost immediately my friend said, "Have you ever considered that thoughts like that are what a victim thinks?" I was taken aback. No one had ever said that to me. I had no realization that was my mindset. He talked to me a while about that and then said, "Are you aware you are assigning a motive to Ron's character when you think that? Have you ever told him what you think and feel in these kinds of conversations?"*

*No, I hadn't. I was fearful of conflict and didn't want to hurt Ron's feelings. But hiding truth and stuffing feelings was not producing good fruit. In my anger and resentment, I carried a grudge, and unspoken words left tension in the air that our guest could sense. The initial "event" that evoked an angry, resentful response from me was then able to be used to guide me toward a healthier way of thinking, feeling and behaving.*

*As I worked through the conversation with my counselor friend, I realized in order to allow the Holy Spirit to grow His fruit, I needed to change. I had a choice. The next time something triggered the victim mentality and feelings of anger and resentment in me, I could be ready with a new thought so I could start to feel differently and behave differently.*

*My new thought? The Holy Spirit said this to me, "Carolyn, it is time to take responsibility for your own feelings and behaviors." He wanted me to learn to challenge my thought system so I would not live life from a victim mentality. He wanted me to be open with Ron (and others in similar situations) and be brave enough to say, "When that just happened, I thought _____ and I felt _____. Is that what you wanted to convey to me?"*

*This insight – that my reactions to Ron's behavior, tone of voice and words that day had more to do with my thoughts and perceptions than his actions – has helped me in all my relationships, to be slow to judge others' intentions and perceptions.*

*God wanted me to quit assigning motives to others without asking them their intentions. I had to consider the truth that others do not get to define who I am. Only God gets to do that. It was time to assume my God-given responsibility for my own choices. (A hard lesson to learn when for all my life I had habituated myself in the way a victim thinks.). With the Holy Spirit's help, though, I changed! I first had to recognize the lie I believed and choose to change, and I had the help I needed to start the process.*

That experience started me on an intentional journey to change that victim mindset to one of a conqueror who lives from a stance of victory. As I listened to my inner dialogue, I began to notice that when I asked certain questions, I ended up in an endless loop of negativity. I needed to see another perspective and trust that there was a redemptive solution to get out of that destructive cycle.

Most of my questions had been directed at my mistakes, failures, and sometimes sin. I was really good at condemning myself and not so good at receiving the gifts Jesus provided for me when He died on the cross. My condemning questions sounded like:

Why do I keep doing these stupid things?

What is wrong with me?

What is wrong with _____? Why don't *they* ever change?

Whose fault is this? (Someone has to pay…justice must be done.)

Will I *ever* get this right?

These questions invariably left me thinking I was a failure with no hope of changing. They left me feeling alone, discouraged, defeated, shamed, and condemned.

## LEARNING TO REHEARSE THE TRUTH OF WHO GOD SAYS WE ARE IS IMPORTANT.

Learning to rehearse the truth of who God says we are is important. There is a helpful list of these truths in Appendix D. While this list establishes a great foundation from which to work, we also need to learn how to *apply* the truths of who we are in Christ. Part of doing this is paying attention to our inner dialogue and changing our questions about life to ones that will lead us to discover God's thoughts and ways.

Can you hear yourself having this kind of interchange? What are some of the ways you habituate yourself in/with negative questions that keep you from seeing possible solutions? Questions such as these and many others did not leave room for me to be on a path to see what possibilities the Lord was offering to me. It was difficult for me to engage in the kinds of discovery questions we will learn about in the next chapter. Even questions I would ask the Lord, genuinely expecting an answer, left me with unsettled results.

Many of us have heard the saying that insanity is doing the same thing over and over but expecting different results. Well, I definitely wanted different results in my life, so I needed to *do* something different – and that something different was to learn how to ask the right kinds of questions. I set out on a path to learn how to recognize self-condemning, shaming and judgmental questions. As I did, I could then change those questions to discovery questions. We will explore the process of repositioning ourselves by refocusing from condemnation to discovery. I didn't realize how much of my self-talk was condemning – of myself, others, and even of God. Jesus had something better for me and I was ready for it.

Besides the questions mentioned previously, other common condemning questions are: Why should I even bother anymore? I always get it wrong anyway.

Why is it never enough?

Why try?

Why are other people always blocking me?

Why doesn't someone notice me? Why am I always left out?

Why doesn't God ever hear me or heal me or answer me or...?

## CONDEMNING QUESTIONS ARE LAW-BASED, PERSONALITY-FOCUSED, AND PROBLEM-ORIENTED.

As we start to recognize condemning questions, we can begin to reflect:

- Is this question producing a desirable line of thinking, feeling and behaving?

- Is this question based on a set of rules? Is it legalistic? Or is it based on the law of love?

- Is this question centered on who I think I am? Who I think God is? Who I think someone else is? Or is it focused on the issue that needs to be considered?

- Is this question leading me to blame someone else for what has gone wrong? Or does it enable me to look at my own thoughts and behavior so I can accept responsibility for them?

Personality-focused questions usually lead to condemnation, shaming, and judging. They will usually end in an argument, going head-to-head with someone. Someone will need to win and someone will need to lose. It is so much more helpful to focus on an issue and connect heart to heart for the benefit of everyone.

The resulting fruit of condemning questions is pessimism, stress, limitations, judgments, inflexibility, reacting versus responding, disconnecting, defensiveness, and reverting to attack mode.

## CLARITY AND REVELATION ARE NEVER RESULTS OF CONDEMNATION.

Condemning questions always end in an overall culture of confusion, oppression, and doubt. Clarity and revelation are never results of condemnation.

Condemning questions release toxins in our body and drain us physically and emotionally. This decreases our ability to use our energies to make good choices.[9]

Learning to recognize those condemning questions is a huge step toward changing our lives. As we begin asking better questions, we will be amazed at the answers we receive and how our new mindset and actions gain the power to change our way of living. So let's use our energy to move forward on the path to discovery. Are you as ready as I am for this?

# Jen's Story

I became a Christian when I was twenty-two. I was surrounded by amazing people who had known Jesus for much longer than I. They wanted to see me grow and flourish, and one of the questions they asked me the most was "What is your passion?" They wanted me to plug in and live in my giftings and calling. It's not a bad thing to want for people, but I thought I couldn't be honest and just answer "I don't know." Even worse, I didn't know how to find out.

So I just went about my life, serving at my church and volunteering wherever I was needed, going through seasons where I did it all and seasons where I did nothing. I felt shame for not knowing my passion. I loved being a wife and mom, but that didn't seem to fit the criteria for "passion." It seemed that I really didn't have an identity at church. I was just the one who always knew what was going on and could answer most questions from an operations standpoint.

Because of these feelings and thoughts, I shied away from praying for people, never considered that I could hear a prophetic word from God, and hid from being in the spotlight in any way.

When I was forty-seven, I was invited to participate in a cohort at church for leaders. The question of passion came up and I froze. In our small group of seven people, there would be nowhere to hide. But then something happened. Carolyn asked the question differently. She said "What is your woe is me? Woe is me if I don't _____."

Suddenly, the answer to this question began to flow on paper. I was hearing very clearly from the Lord! When I was done writing, I knew that not only was my passion written down for the first time in twenty-five years, but I was also already actively participating in it. I was overwhelmed with joy. All it took was six little words in the form of a question to open me up, erase the shame and change my thoughts.

I will forever be grateful for this question and the way it changed my perspective. I make sure to suggest it to people who are struggling with knowing their own calling, giftings, passion and purpose. Sometimes all it takes is the right question to unlock what God has placed within you.

Jen Skaggs

# CHAPTER SIX:

## *Discovery Questions*

IN THE EARLY 1970S PASTOR RON ALLEN ATTENDED a seminar at Purdue University, where he heard a speaker named Peter Drucker present on Management by Objective (MBO). Ron was intrigued by the presentation and the thoughts he heard that day. One of the statements that stuck like an arrow in his mind was, "Goals are not set but discovered." Ron adapted that statement to ministry and for years has said, "For the believer, goals are not set; they are discovered."

> FOR THE BELIEVER, GOALS ARE NOT SET;
> THEY ARE DISCOVERED.

Putting that concept into practice as a believer has been a default position through many years of leading a local congregation on a path of discovery for both personal and community identity. If we are serious about following the guidance of the Holy Spirit for our lives, we don't have the option to set our own goals. As we listen to Him (through reading the Word and dialoguing with Him and each other), we obey – and walk out His purposes for our lives.

It has been an adventure to listen, learn, and lead, discovering new life rather than leaving possibilities unfulfilled because of a negative, self-condemning mindset.

As I have applied this principle to the art of asking questions in ministry, it has led to the practice of formulating questions designed to take us on a path of discovery with the Holy Spirit. These questions are so powerful they can determine our destination. Will we train ourselves to ask the Lord questions that allow us to hear His possibilities and solutions? Or will we continue to ask and listen to answers that sabotage us and keep us on the path (described in chapter four) that leads to doubt, deception, disobedience and death?

## DISCOVERY QUESTIONS OPEN THE DOOR TO FREEDOM.

Discovery questions open the door to freedom. Some discovery questions one can ask in almost any situation are:

"Lord Jesus, what do You want for me in this situation?"

"Lord Jesus, what will work in this situation?"

"Lord Jesus, what perspective do You want me to adopt about this so I can walk in freedom?"

"Lord Jesus, what do You want me to learn from this?"

"Lord Jesus, what options would You like for me to consider?"

"Lord Jesus, how will changing my perspective to agree with You change my behavior?"

"Lord Jesus, what are the possibilities/solutions about this for me to consider?"

"Lord Jesus, who do You want to be for me in and through this situation?"

"Lord Jesus, what will help me be aware when I am facing this situation again? Would you help me be aware of the familiar thoughts, feelings or behaviors that cause me to return to old habit patterns?"

## DISCOVERY QUESTIONS ARE LOVE-BASED, ISSUE-FOCUSED AND SOLUTION-ORIENTED.

In light of these principles, as we begin implementing discovery questions, we can keep on the right track by asking:

- Is this question based on love or fear?

- Does this question relate to the central issue with which I am struggling? What needs to be addressed?

- Will this question lead me to a solution or keep me on a path of self-condemnation and judgment (of myself, others, or God)?

Using discovery questions results in optimism, hope, possibilities uncovered, understanding, flexibility, relationship, connection, and collaboration. All of these are qualities of the Lord Jesus. It is part of the culture, if you will, of a Kingdom of God orientation. Since the Father's goal is to transform us from glory to glory to look like His Son Jesus Christ (1 Corinthians 3:18), these are some of the qualities we want to reach for on our journey. Asking the right questions enables us to progress to that end.

If a question is based on love, there will be a resulting sense of peace, empowerment, acceptance, trust, and hope.

Sometimes we find ourselves wrestling with several issues at the same time. Singling out one concern to address will enable us to ask relevant questions and hear more clearly. We can put aside the others for another time with a set of questions pertinent to them. This exercise also empowers us to focus on the issue and not our failures, weaknesses or personality quirks. While God may want to deal with some of those, He will do it on an issue-by-issue basis, not a storm thrown at us to overwhelm us. Focusing on a single issue will help us craft our questions accordingly.

When asking a discovery question, it is helpful to lay aside any assumptions or expectations that could hinder us from hearing something new. Saying something like, "Lord Jesus, I have a pretty strong opinion about this, but so far the results of my having this opinion have not been good. So I am willing to lay my thoughts down and ask You to reveal Your thoughts and solutions to my situation. I am ready to hear Your way. What is Your perspective on this issue?" This repositions us to a discovery frame of mind, flexible and ready to receive what could be an innovative revelation.

## DISCOVERY QUESTIONS ARE INVITATIONAL TO NEW IDEAS BY DESIGN.

We need to keep in mind the possibility that what we have been thinking and basing our life on could be wrong. Adopting this stance allows humility to be at work through our thought processes. We must be transparent, willing to receive new ways of thinking in order to be transformed, and receptive to the reality, "I don't have the answer and I don't know what it is, but God does." Author Marilee Adams frames it this way: "To value not-knowing is the basis of learning and all creativity and innovation."[10] Discovery questions are invitational to new ideas by design.

When we ask discovery questions, we focus on our relationship with God, hearing Him and learning what fruit He is growing in our lives. We're not focusing so much on changing our behavior as we are enjoying the process of deepening the intimacy we have with God. We learn how much we are loved and accepted. Hope rises as we hear Him speak truth to us.

Hope that God *will* speak to us and God *will* transform us, completing what He began, carries us through transformative seasons. The Holy Spirit enables us to have soft hearts that are flexible and willing to change. Learning to think new thoughts that release different emotions and behaviors is a challenge – one that is life-changing when we say "Yes" to the process.

Are you ready to say "Yes" and learn how to refocus your questions from condemnation to discovery?

# Jordan's Story

When I was nineteen, I struggled heavily with depression. I had recently dropped out of college and felt very lost. I had absolutely no confidence in myself and struggled with feelings of loneliness and abandonment. I wrestled with the idea of God, thinking that if He does exist, He must not like me or be very kind. Out of all the people in the world, there was one person on whom I thought I could rely. That person was my brother. We had been through many hard things together, and I always thought I could talk to him and felt he understood me.

One day we made the terrible realization that we had feelings for the same girl. My brother, who I trusted and hoped would support me as I worked up the courage to ask her out, quickly became my nemesis. He started doing whatever he could to belittle me or make me look bad in front of her. My heart filled with rage.

That summer, I started a dirty and physically demanding job, making just over minimum wage. I worked long, hard hours hand cleaning a 100,000 square foot metal roof building that had recently caught fire. Summer temperatures soared and I would finish each day exhausted and covered in soot, looking like a coal miner. I came home after work one day, struggling with the thought of where my life was heading. That's when I saw my brother. The sight of him so angered me I just turned right around and went to sit in my car.

I will never forget sitting in the front passenger seat with my eyes full of tears knowing that I was at my breaking point. Not knowing what else to do, I wondered if I should take a chance on God. With my last fragment of faith, I asked Him, "What will it take for me to not feel this way anymore?"

To my surprise, the Lord spoke to me, and with one word, He shook me to my core. He said, "Seek." My body trembled under that word, and it was as if every demonic force in my life ran away in fear, and every ounce of depression was gone. The anger toward my brother vanquished and I felt captivated in such a holy moment.

I thought that maybe I was going crazy, but I told the Lord, "I'll start going to church, and I'll read the Bible. Where do you want me to read?"

He told me, "Read James."

So, I went and found a Bible. Relieved that there even was a book of James, I read how to have joy through suffering. I read about loving God during trials. I read about being a doer and not just a hearer. All of it hit me square in the chest. And then I came across a beautiful promise in James 4:8: "Draw near to God, and He will draw near to you." I don't know if I ever felt more loved and comforted to know that I wasn't alone and I could have as much of the Lord as I wanted. I just had to ask.

Asking that question put me in a posture to discover that I wasn't on my own. Even now, after more than sixteen years, I look back on that moment and I'm filled with deep, heartfelt gratitude. It was as if the love of God was so hot that it branded me and left a permanent mark on my life. It launched me in a new direction and became one of the most dynamic and spiritually intimate summers of my entire life. I continued to have conversations with the Lord and to make discovery after discovery of the goodness of God.

Jordan Numbers

# CHAPTER SEVEN:

## *Refocusing Questions*
## *Repositioning from Condemnation*
## *to Discovery*

ONE OF THE MOST POWERFUL GIFTS GIVEN TO us as children of God is the power to choose. When we use this gift and choose to change our life course direction, we must often learn to change the focus of our questions.

A favorite "Ronism" (as quotes from my husband are fondly known) is this:

> *"God's way is the best way. You're free to choose any way you want, but you are not free to avoid the consequences of what you choose."*

So true.

I detail the skill of recognizing thinking that is destroying our lives in my book *Journey into Wholeness* (available on Amazon.com), so I won't talk about that here. Just know that if we can change our thoughts to change our lives, we can go a step farther: we can change our questions to hear better answers to meet the end goal of a healthy, fruitful life.

## WE STAND AT A CROSSROADS EVERY TIME WE CHOOSE A THOUGHT.

We stand at a crossroads every time we choose a thought. We must learn to quickly ask ourselves, "What thought will I choose to accept as a truth on which to live my life?" We choose the fruit we want growing in our life when we ask questions in the decision-making process. Will we choose a path that leads to condemnation and shame, or will we choose a path of discovery led by the Holy Spirit?

We often find ourselves facing challenging, confusing situations because we believe ungodly thoughts. Since we always live out what we are thinking, the resulting fruit is not Christlike. *Fundamental change often depends on first asking better or different questions.* The world of inner questioning is the soil in which grow the fears, concerns, beliefs, and hopes that drive us. The Apostle Paul struggled with this as well, as evidenced by his asking, "Why do I keep doing the things I don't want to do?" (Romans 7:15-25)

Many of the questions we ask, both consciously and subconsciously, lie at the source of our discontent and confusion. When we learn to ask better questions, we arrive at a different destination.

"Research shows that 75 to 98 percent of mental, physical, and behavioral illness comes from one's thought life. This staggering and eye-opening statistic means only 2 to 25 percent of mental and physical illnesses come from the environment and genes."[11]

"What you wire into your brain through thinking is stored in your nonconscious mind. The nonconscious mind is where 99.9 percent of our mind activity is. It is the root level that stores the thoughts with the emotions and perceptions, and it impacts the conscious mind and what we say and do. Everything is first a thought."[12]

An interesting passage of Scripture talks about choosing a path. Through the prophet Jeremiah the Lord spoke to the people of Judah, who had rejected God's ways and warnings. He sent Jeremiah with more warnings and instructions, presenting this choice:

*The Lord said: "You are standing at the crossroads. So consider your path. Ask where the old, reliable paths are. Ask where the path is that leads to blessing and follow it. If you do, you will find rest for your souls." But they said, "We will not follow it!" (Jeremiah 6:16 NET)*

This is very sad to me. We all do this, sometimes intentionally, sometimes unintentionally – but the result is the same. When we are at a crossroads (every time we choose a thought), we are to stop and consider what path to take. We are to ask where the Godly, trustworthy paths are – the ones we can count on because they were ordained by God and lead to blessing and discovery with God. That is where we find rest for our souls – mind, will and emotions. That is what we desperately need! The inner dialogue of condemning questions wears us out! But Jesus invites us to come to Him when we are weary. He is the One who will give us rest for our souls (Matthew 11:28-30).

## PAL: PAUSE, ASK, LISTEN

So we PAL: Pause, Ask, Listen. "God, what is the path You want me to take? What is the thought You want me to adopt about this situation? About this person? That's the path I want to take because I desperately need rest from all this confusion and doubt."

What path will you choose? When you are at a crossroads, you can reposition yourself anytime by asking different questions!

As an example, Ron and I were traveling home with a newborn from a first-time visit to Grandpa and Grandma's house. He fell ill and I needed to drive, even though I had not fully recovered from our daughter's difficult birth and was very weak. It was late at night and we were both exhausted. Ron went to sleep and when he awoke, he saw a sign that said, "Cincinnati 100 miles." He shouted, "We're on the wrong road! What happened?" We were supposed to be headed home to New Castle, Indiana, but somehow at an interchange in Indianapolis I took the wrong road. It was raining hard and with trucks on both sides of us, I had missed seeing the correct sign. (This was before the days of GPS.) We needed to stop and reconfigure a route that would enable us to get home. We began to ask a series of questions to meet that goal.

Some unhelpful questions that came first were, "What did you do? Do you know how far off course we are now? How did this happen?" Those questions did not help us get on the right road toward home, however. Instead, they just flooded me with feelings of shame and self- condemnation. Tired and frustrated, I thought: "How did I get us in this mess? Why can't I do this right?"

We finally made a choice to change those questions to some that would give us better answers. "Where are we?" "Where is the nearest road to get turned around?" "How long will this take?" We began to think about the situation differently and got on the right road. It wasn't long before we started having some good laughs about our situation.

> ## "...ASKING THE RIGHT QUESTIONS MAY BE THE MOST IMPORTANT PART OF THINKING."
> Edward de Bono

In his book *Six Thinking Hats*, Edward de Bono said, "Asking a question is the simplest way of focusing thinking…asking the right question may be the most important part of thinking."[13]

It takes time to retrain the brain to think a different way. Dr. Caroline Leaf has done extensive research on the brain's function and what it takes to rewire it to think a new way. Asking condemning and judgmental questions fills our minds with toxic thinking. When that happens, our ability to process information is greatly affected. Too many toxins released in our body result in physical, emotional and spiritual disease.[14]

The questions we ask, and the resulting conclusions, affect our brains negatively or positively. They cause us to embrace either toxic thoughts or Godly thoughts – with drastically different results.

"So, when we make a poor-quality decision – when we choose to engage toxic thoughts (for example, unforgiveness, bitterness, irritation, or feelings of not coping) – we change the DNA and subsequent genetic expression, which then changes the shape of our brain wiring in a negative direction."[15]

## WE HAVE THE POWER TO CHOOSE OUR THOUGHTS BY CHANGING OUR QUESTIONS.

Condemning questions require more energy to ask and answer. They drain us emotionally. What would it be like to redirect our energy and brain-power and ask discovery questions instead? Discovery questions are good for our mental, emotional, spiritual, and physical health. Asking discovery questions invites the Holy Spirit to answer the questions He wants to use to impart God's wisdom for our journey. Remember – we have the power to choose our thoughts by changing our questions.

Learning to change our questions to a discovery path will enable us to move into the freedom of walking in the Spirit. Some call this a paradigm shift. When we reposition ourselves from negative habitual patterns of thought to Godly thinking, we are being transformed by renewing our minds (Romans 12:2). Appendix E is an Activation Worksheet that walks you through the 5 "Rs" leading to transformed thinking:

- Recognize the lie you have believed and on which you have based your life.

- Repent for believing the lie. Ask the Holy Spirit to help you write a Godly belief.

- Renew your mind according to this fresh insight from God through:

- Repetition and

- Rehearsal

You can know when you need to consider asking a different question by looking at the fruit of what you have been asking and thinking. Is the fruit of your behavior full of love, joy, peace, patience, kindness, goodness, faithfulness, gentleness, and self-control? Are you at peace or in confusion and turmoil? Are you walking in freedom or bondage? Are you walking in the Spirit or in the flesh (from your own thoughts, feelings and willpower)?

Walking in anything less than what Jesus promised and provided for us is a sign we most likely need to re-evaluate our inner dialogue (our questions) and thinking. Knowing who Jesus is in, for and through us is necessary for developing Christ-like thoughts and behavior. Knowing who He says we are because of His presence indwelling us is just as important.

In Appendices C and D I have included the lists "Christ in Me Is…" and "In Christ …" for your devotions and meditation. Internalizing these truths about Christ and yourself will change the way you think, feel, and behave. They hold the ingredients necessary for transformation – the goal of our Heavenly Father (2 Corinthians 3:18).

*Learning to change our inner dialogue/questions as soon as a pattern is recognized is a key to transformation.* As we develop more awareness that we want to change our inner dialogue, here are some questions that can help us focus. Different questions precede different results.

- Am I still on the right path? Am I moving in a helpful direction?

- What is the issue here?

- Am I engaging in either/or thinking?

- What assumptions am I making that could get in the way?

- Am I confusing what is going on with my feelings about what is taking place?

- Is the way I'm thinking making me feel worse or better? What is the fruit?

- How else can I think about this situation?

- What can I learn from this?

- What are my choices/options?

- What choice would be effective and affirming and help me move beyond this?

## CHANGE "WHO'S TO BLAME?" QUESTIONS TO "WHAT IS MY RESPONSIBILITY IN THIS SITUATION?"

Change "Who's to blame?" questions to "What is my responsibility in this situation?" Instead of judging others or yourself, you'll discover a path that will enable you to take responsibility for your thoughts and actions with the help of the Holy Spirit.

Here are some other examples of how to refocus condemning questions to discovery questions:

- Not this: What's wrong with me?

  But this: Jesus, is there another way for me to think about this so I can agree with You?

- Not this: Why do I always do the wrong thing?

But this: Jesus, what do You want me to learn from this?

- Not this: Why am I so stupid?

  But this: Jesus, who do You want to be in/for/through me in this?

- Not this: Why even bother anymore?

  But this: Jesus, I'm so discouraged and want to quit because I seem to get the same results every time. What am I missing that You want me to see to have a different outcome?

- Not this: Why is he/she so _____?

  But this: Jesus, what are some of the judgments I have made about him/her that have led me to this thought?

- Not this: Why try when I know I can't do this?

  But this: Jesus, when you look at this situation, what do You think? Is it true that I can't do this? What do You say?

- Not this: Why are others (is _____) always blocking me?

  But this: Jesus, what consequences am I living out today as a result of this situation? As a result of this person's words/actions?

Is it time to re-evaluate your lifestyle and relationships because you are noticing ungodly fruit? Perhaps it is time to look at the questions and thoughts you have and refocus to some Holy Spirit-led discovery questions. Discovery with Him is always an adventure!

# Dave's Story

I was in the midst of teaching through a sermon series on worship at Heartland Church. We were well into the series, and my passion for preaching on this subject was growing week after week. I was very excited to get the Lord's direction for the upcoming weekend, so on Monday I asked Him a question: "Lord, what message about worship do You want me to preach Sunday?" The days went by with no answer from the Lord. By Thursday I was starting to get a little nervous and I began wondering why I wasn't hearing an answer. I was persistent though, and kept asking Him the same question and putting myself in a posture of listening.

## IF THE LORD'S NOT ANSWERING THE QUESTION YOU'RE ASKING... CHANGE YOUR QUESTION.

Saturday came and I still didn't have an answer. As my frustration grew, I began to wonder what the Lord was doing. Suddenly I remembered a statement Carolyn had made: "If the Lord's not answering the question you're asking... change your question." I realized the Lord was reminding me of her statement, so I decided to ask Him a different question. I went to a place of prayer and said, "Lord, what message do you want me to preach on Sunday?" (Notice how this time I left out the words 'about worship'?) Instantly I heard the Lord say, "Preach on healing."

That answer changed my plans and the sermon series I was on, but it was a clear answer that I was eager to receive.

The next day at Heartland, I shared this story and preached on healing. I received some incredible testimonies from people who needed to hear that word from the Lord on that day. I am so thankful for Carolyn's teaching that has shaped my prayer life so powerfully.

Dave Frincke

# CHAPTER EIGHT:

## *Ministry Focused Questions*

### *For Ministry Facilitators*

"PLEASE, I DESPERATELY NEED HELP. I'VE TRIED medicine, psychologists, psychiatrists, self-help books, prayer, counseling – you name it, I've tried it. Nothing is working for me. I'm here to see you as my last stop. If you can't help me, I have no place to go. Fix me." Tears are flowing and you can see a deep pain resident in the eyes. People are desperate for help. People are desperate for hope. People are desperate for something to change.

What would you say to this desperate person?

Endeavoring to be a facilitator in someone's healing journey can be a challenging experience. Remembering that people are not projects but human beings who have hurts, wounds, disappointments, joys, and valleys is vital. It is also crucial to remember we cannot fix anyone – we are not the answer to anyone's problem. We are not the power source of anyone's healing. That role belongs to the Holy Spirit Who works in and through people's lives. When we direct our questions to the Lord, a critical safeguard is in place to prevent us from taking on responsibility for someone else's challenges.

With that in mind, God *does* desire to use each of us to encourage, edify, comfort, challenge, and direct people to Jesus for wisdom and life.

One of the passages of Scripture that guides my life and ministry is from Colossians 1:28-29 (MSG):

*We proclaim Jesus Christ, admonishing every man and teaching every man with all wisdom, so that we may present every man complete in Christ. For this purpose also I labor, striving according to His power, which mightily works within me.*

This Scripture helps me keep on track. I am hopeful for a fruitful return on the investment I make in people while using His power, wisdom and anointing. He initiates, we participate with Him, and we enjoy seeing the results worked out in a precious life.

For me, nothing is more powerful than seeing the light bulb come on for someone who has just heard the Lord speak a revelatory word to them about their situation. Time and time again, I have seen the Holy Spirit speak in creative ways that were tailor-made for them. Freedom truly does come from the Lord for each one of us. "Where the Spirit of the Lord is, there is freedom" (2 Corinthians 3:17).

Two of the main reasons we ask questions in ministry are that we need information and want to help connect people with Jesus. When we ask for information, we may need clarification. This is not a time for a relationship-building conversation. Staying focused on a single issue will enable a fruitful outcome of the time spent with the person. Questions can help clarify, focus, and refocus the information necessary to move ahead with the ministry the Holy Spirit wants to accomplish.

Knowing the focus of the issue helps guide the choice for the questions we use to direct people to the Lord. One of the first activations we do with the participant (person who comes for prayer ministry) is to help them craft a focus statement. This statement describes why they are seeking help. It defines a habitual pattern of thought, feeling and behavior and enables the participant to stay on target as they complete their assessment. It also guides the ministry team as they pray and develop a Holy Spirit-led strategy to begin the journey of healing.

Charles Kettering, inventor and head of research for GM, said, "A problem well-stated is a problem half-solved."[16] Well-crafted focus statements enhance the development of a Spirit-led ministry plan. Learning to use the focus statement to ask questions opens the mind to possible solutions. Every time we ask the question from a different perspective, we are presented with more options to consider.

Let's look at a situation from a person's life followed by unclear versus well-crafted focus statements. As an example, a person has lost their job and consequently their way of functioning in everyday life.

The following focus statement is unclear and will not enable them or the team to stay on target as they design a ministry plan.

> "I feel like I'm a total mess up. Nothing I do turns out right. I feel like I'm always on the wrong side of right and I hate my life. I just lost my job and I'm sure it's because someone else messed up and blamed me. How can I ever hope to be anything?"

Feelings and thoughts are not distinct, making it challenging to identify specific thoughts, feelings and behaviors. Most of the attempts at sharing feelings are thoughts. When the word "feel" is coupled with "like" it is usually a thought, not a feeling. No behaviors are identified that will strengthen the planning and transformation process.

A well-crafted focus statement might read, "When I think about losing my job, I feel depressed, anxious and fearful because I think I am a failure. I am worthless. When I dwell on this, I withdraw and isolate myself from everyone and everything." This statement includes thoughts, feelings and behaviors:

- Thoughts: I am a failure. I am worthless.

- Feelings: I feel depressed, anxious, and fearful.

- Behaviors: I withdraw and isolate.

We consider all of these elements as we minister to people. We need to know what they are thinking and believing because their thoughts release emotions that produce behavior. Trying to change behavior before thoughts or feelings might be successful for a time, but the behavior will return as it is born from a thought pattern. That is how we are created. Romans 12:2 instructs us to be transformed by renewing our mind – not our feelings, not our behavior – our mind.

## "WHAT THOUGHT RELEASES THIS EMOTION?"

## "WHAT THOUGHT PRODUCES THIS TYPE OF BEHAVIOR?"

To discern thoughts and feelings, we can PAL: "What thought releases this emotion?" "What thought produces this type of behavior?"

As believers and ministers, we must remember the goal of asking our questions: facilitating a path of discovery and connecting with Jesus Christ. Are we hoping for redemption, restoration, reconciliation, and restitution? Do we have a win/win mindset rather than a win/lose mindset?

We are continually helping participants shift from asking condemning questions to discovery questions as we facilitate their prayers. When a condemning question is asked, we gently suggest, "How about we ask it this way?" and continue with the prayer.

As we craft a question, we can challenge our motivation for asking with this PAL: "What is the reason I am asking this question? Do I need to know this?"

If we are honest with ourselves, sometimes we ask a question to point out the error in someone else's thinking or behavior. Or we want to make ourselves look superior because we 'caught' them thinking or doing something wrong. We like to be right – and let it be known we are right. Sometimes we ask because we are curious, but the information we glean has nothing to do with the issue at hand. If we are not careful, we can be quick to point out character flaws and judge people. Matthew 7:5 has a caution for us in this regard: "Hypocrite! First take the log out of your own eye, and then you will see clearly to take the speck out of your brother's eye!"

Questions can be manipulative and used to control a response. However, while we may recognize the participant is embracing an ungodly belief (murder *is* a sin, sexual immorality *is* a sin, etc.), we desire to enable them to hear the truth from God. Encouraging a PAL or a study will empower them to discover God's truth so they can 'own' it as a principle they will use to guide their life. We must guard against using questions to get someone to agree with our opinion about something.

We will continue exploring ministry-focused questions with scenarios and PAL examples in the next chapter.

# Chris's Story

"I'm going to ask you three questions, and then we're going to have to figure out if this is the right place for you."

I was three months into a Christian rehab program for sex addicts. Just a few months before, I had blown up my life, family, ministry, marriage, and reputation as details of a deep addiction to lust and pornography were discovered. I should've been broken, ashamed, humbled, and contrite. But instead, I went to rehab thinking I knew all the answers. I was in ministry, after all. I'd helped other men through this struggle. I even knew the Bible better than my counselor, Brad.

"I'm just not getting through to you," Brad said, after he threatened to kick me out. He pointed out to me that for a guy who knew all the answers, I sure had made a mess of my life. And he was right.

His threat was real, and he said if I couldn't come up with honest answers to his questions, my time there was done.

"First, why do you look for ways — little and big — to rebel and skirt your way around the rules? Next, why are you always judging everyone around you? And third, and this is the most important one, Chris...what do you really want right now? From this, from life, from God, from everything... what do you want?"

I left and went directly to the chapel. I couldn't bear having to face everyone back home and admit I had failed at rehab, too. I took those questions to the Lord, pleading with Him to show me the answers I needed. Over the course of the next twelve hours, God answered in spades. That night, he answered the second question first in a dream.

*Why are you always judging everyone?* The details of the dream are long, drawn out, and not important. What is important is the actual answer: I judge everyone because I think everyone is judging me. In my dream, God showed me how I am afraid of others and concerned about what they think of me. I was the kind of person Jesus was talking to in Matthew 10:28: "And do not be afraid of those who kill the body but are unable to kill the soul; but rather fear Him who is able to destroy both soul and body in hell." I was afraid of people more than I was afraid of God.

*Why do you look for ways to rebel and skirt your way around the rules?* The next question was answered with such mercy, tenderness, and wisdom. It actually happened in the shower, which I realize now was God's plan all along. He warned me that He was going to answer this for me, and then He "peeled back" a corner of my heart. I'd come from a Christian circle that didn't really know how to handle Jeremiah saying our hearts are "wicked and deceitful" (17:9). I had bought into a cheap gospel that made MUCH of self. I thought I was basically good inside. Maybe I didn't teach it like that, but I believed it. God revealed just a little corner, and I was immediately overcome with anger, greed, intense selfishness, rage, suicidal thoughts, and all kinds of evil. It was maybe two or three seconds, but it seemed like many minutes. For perhaps the first time in my life, I began to see what I was really like without Jesus. His mercy in that moment was this: I was alone. In just those few seconds, I was full of so much hate for others and myself that all I wanted to do was cause harm. Two seconds in the shower didn't leave much room for that!

*What do you really want right now?* Of all the questions, this was the hardest. After realizing the fear of man I walked in, and how dark and evil I was at my core, there was only one conclusion to this. A few days later I slumped in the spare chair in Brad's office and told him that when he heard the answer to this last one, he would kick me out. I was sure of it. "What I really want right now, I mean *really want*, is my addiction. I want my sin. I *don't* want to be free." I began crying, ashamed that the pain I had caused myself and my family wasn't enough to motivate me to change.

When I looked up a few moments later, Brad was smiling. "Chris, you've been here three months and that's the first time you've admitted that truth out loud. NOW the program can begin."

During the ten months I spent in a seven-month rehab, I learned the value of heart-searching questions that required me to be honest. While it was painful to answer those questions, the results for me continue to be life-changing.

Chris Ishak

# CHAPTER NINE:

## *Ministry Focused Questions: Scenarios*

***For Ministry Facilitators***

THE SCENARIOS PRESENTED IN THIS CHAPTER
will allow you to see specific examples that frequently happen as you minister. You can adapt the questions/prayers to your situation.

*Scenario*: One of the guidelines I endeavor to utilize is to avoid using "why" questions because they tend to put people on the defensive. Rather than say something like, "Why are you behaving like that?" Or, "Why are you acting like such a jerk?" it would be more helpful and redemptive to say something like this: "I hear you say \_\_\_\_\_, but I see you \_\_\_\_\_ (behavior). Something doesn't quite line up for me. Can you help me understand what you are thinking? Do you see this happening in your life?"

The nature of the conversation can change depending on what questions you ask, your tone of voice, and body posture. You will save yourself time and frustration if you learn to keep your questions on the focus statement, keeping in mind the end goal of redemption and restoration by staying on a path of discovery.

*Scenario*: What do you do when the participant has trouble seeing any good in themselves? This contributing factor is often present when a person's life seems to be a series of traumatic events that have resulted in confusion, broken relationships and a lack of hope that anything will ever go right for them.

Here is a gentle PAL prayer you can use:

> "Lord Jesus, I'm here because I desperately need help. My life is a mess. I think I must be a mistake or a horrible person because nothing ever seems to turn out right for me. I feel hopeless and helpless right now. When You created me in my mother's womb, what character qualities did you have in mind for me? What purpose did you have in mind for my life? I'm struggling to find answers that make sense. Would you help me today?

> "I have read it in the Bible and heard people talk about how we are loved, chosen and have a purpose, but I don't see those results in my life. I need to hear this from You and know it so I can be free. Can I give you this hopelessness and the situations in my life today? What do you want to say to me about me right now?"

## HOW WILL THIS TRUTH CHANGE MY BEHAVIOR?

After leading this prayer, sit and listen with them. Give them time. As they listen, they may need to soak in what they hear Jesus saying. Appendices C (Christ In Me is…) and D (In Christ I…) are helpful homework to habituate ourselves in these truths. Learning how to walk in them changes our lives. A question that will empower walking in these truths is, "How will this truth change my behavior?"

*Scenario*: When a participant has experienced some type of abuse, it is not uncommon to hear this statement: "I'm not asking for forgiveness for anything. I didn't do anything wrong. They did. I'm not praying this prayer!"

The part of the prayer to which they are reacting is, "Lord Jesus, would you forgive me for my sin of any ungodly thought patterns I adopted and embraced as a result of what _____ said/did to me? I repent for living out these lies. Would you please forgive me?" You likely will not get past "Would you forgive me for my sin?" as the reaction is intense. A teaching moment has just been presented. The person is about to learn the importance of taking responsibility for their thoughts, feelings and behavior in response to the sin committed against them. They have just forgiven the person for what has been done. Now they are asking for forgiveness from God for the ungodly fruit developed in their life as a result of a thought pattern adopted that didn't agree with God. Sometimes it can take several conversations for this revelation to come; it is about personal responsibility for thoughts, feelings and behavior and allowing the Holy Spirit to convict, forgive and cleanse them as they are transformed.

A great question to PAL here might be, "As a result of what was said and done to me, what thought pattern have I embraced that enabled me to live in a manner contrary to Your ways?"

## WHAT WE BELIEVE TO BE TRUE DICTATES OUR BEHAVIOR.

What we believe to be true dictates our behavior. When we disagree with God, we sin against Him and need to ask Him to forgive us so we can get on the right path. This is hard for some people to accept because they haven't learned to separate the sin committed against them from their personal sin of how they responded. Any thought adopted about the person or situation that doesn't agree with God will lead to ungodly behavior. This now becomes a personal responsibility and, when not recognized and embraced, must be challenged.

# HOW LONG DO YOU WANT TO ALLOW YOUR FREEDOM TO BE TIED TO ANOTHER PERSON'S BEHAVIOR AND CHOICES?

If a participant is struggling with forgiving or letting go of judgments about people who have hurt them, asking the following questions helps them think about the consequence that is affecting their life:

How long do you want to allow your freedom to be tied to another person's behavior and choices?

How is it working out for you to hang on to this grudge or bitterness? Are you at peace?

*Scenario*: A participant doesn't see a problem, but you are convinced there is one, and you know what it is. For example, you see the fruit of a judgment in their words and the tone of their voice. This might be evident as hardness in their voice or an attitude of disdain when talking about someone. What do you say to help them see what you see?

An easy fill in the blank statement to reveal if someone has a judgment is, "_____ is _____." Immediately the person thinks of words to describe the person in mind. Sometimes they don't want to say the words because they usually aren't flattering and kind. If they are still hesitant to pray a prayer asking forgiveness for a judgment and opportunity to hear God's perspective of the person, you can ask these questions:

Would you consider that perhaps you have a judgment against this person and pray the prayer with me?

What fruit do you have in your life when you think about this person? Do you experience peace and love, or something negative?

Would you humor me and pray? If there's not a problem, your prayer won't be answered, and nothing will happen. If there is a problem, you will be set free and experience forgiveness and cleansing.

These prayers work with other areas of concern when participants are hesitant to pray because they don't think anything is wrong. When they pray and hear God speak to them, they are delighted you persisted in believing that there was a problem.

> A JUDGMENT IS AN OPINION WE FORM
> WITHOUT ASKING GOD HIS PERSPECTIVE OF
> THE PERSON OR SITUATION.

When working with judgments, we often hear, "But what if the judgment is true?" At times, that is the case: i.e., _____ is harsh, critical and judgmental. This could be true. The point of working through judgments is allowing the Holy Spirit to search our hearts to reveal attitudes that cause us to sin against Him and others. *A judgment is an opinion we form without asking God His perspective of the person or situation.* If someone is harsh, critical and judgmental, the question becomes how God wants us to see them so we can interact with them in a Christlike manner.

Here is a PAL that works: "Lord, I've given you my life. You live in me. The next time I interact with this person, I will choose to let You be who You want to be through me for their well-being. Will You let me know how you are seeing them so I can adopt that mindset instead of thinking of them as harsh, critical and judgmental? When I think that, I get angry and want to stay away from them. I would rather be able to think about them in a way that will produce a Kingdom emotion and Christlike behavior. What would you like to say to me?"

The focus of this PAL is to allow the Holy Spirit to check the attitude of the heart.

Only when we have God's perspective about someone can we interact with and talk about them with kindness when their behavior is still on the journey to becoming Christlike. This reality is true for all of us in some aspect of our being. We are all on a journey, so it's not a helpful exercise to judge others in ways that cause us to produce ungodly fruit.

*Scenario:* A person says something obviously contrary to God's truth.

- I am a mistake. I should never have been born.

- I will never amount to anything. I'll never measure up.

Here are some great questions in response:

- Who told you that?

- Where did you hear that?

- Did someone actually say that to you?

Be aware of the tone of voice and inflection used as you ask these questions. The hearer will hear different questions depending on where the emphasis lies. For example:

"**Who** told you that?" sets the person up to place blame or causes the person to stop and think, "Wait a minute. Who did tell me this? Is it true?"

"Who **told** you that?" reveals an attitude of skepticism. Perhaps the person will hear, "I am foolish for believing this."

"Who told **you** that?" implies they aren't worthy of being told anything. It feels like condescension.

"Who told you **that**?" Think about the substance of the "that." Somebody can ask this question with either consternation or compassion. Compassion will invite the person into hope to consider that the statement might not be accurate. This is an opportunity to PAL, "What does God say is true?"

*Scenario*: A participant is being asked a question for which they don't know the answer. Perhaps during an interview session the person realizes they aren't aware of their family history. Rather than stress about it, PAL, "Lord Jesus, I don't know this information. Is there anything I need to know about this to help me walk in freedom?"

This PAL works if the participant is stuck and can't hear an answer at any time during the ministry: "Lord, I'm stuck and not hearing anything. Do I need to know this, or am I okay to move on?"

*Scenario*: A participant is convinced they don't/can't hear God speaking to them. This can be a challenge, but patience and instruction often break down the barriers. Sometimes the person is hearing but doesn't recognize that God is speaking to them.

Jesus said, "If anyone is thirsty, let him come to Me and drink. The one who believes in Me, as the Scripture said, 'From his innermost being will flow rivers of living water'" (John 7:37-38).

When we believe in Jesus Christ, we have rivers of living water that flow from our innermost being. This flow is the work of the Holy Spirit releasing life, creativity and everything else we need to walk as a new creation. We experience spontaneity that comes from His nature. This is how He delights to communicate with His children.

> "Hearing God's voice is as simple as quieting yourself down,
> fixing your eyes on Jesus, tuning to spontaneity and writing.
> Stillness – Vision – Spontaneity – Journaling"[17]

The ministry facilitator can share different ways we can experience hearing God's voice:

- hearing the audible voice (this seems to be rare)
- hearing or receiving spontaneous thoughts of instruction, comfort, encouragement, or correction

- hearing or having a Scripture spontaneously light upon your mind

- hearing or having a song spontaneously begin playing in your mind

- seeing or having pictures, visions or words light upon your mind

- smelling aromas for which there are no natural explanations

- feeling a sense of peace or comfort that wasn't present before

- tasting a flavor for no apparent reason

As you can see, all five senses are described in how people can recognize the "voice" of the Lord. Many get confused as they listen to other people tell their stories of hearing God speak to them and then think they must hear in the same way. This is a trick of the enemy to convince them they can't/don't hear from God.

An activation that can help some people is to have the person sing "Happy Birthday" or a familiar song in their head without verbalizing or audibly singing. Ask them if they heard the tune and either saw or heard the words as they "sang" the song. Whether the person sees or hears the words can be a clue as to how they will hear the Lord speaking to them. When you craft questions for them, it is helpful to ask, "Did you *hear* the Lord say anything?" or "What thought just crossed your mind?" Or for those who seem to connect by seeing, ask, "Did you *see* anything in answer to the question we just asked Him?" or "What picture lit upon your mind?"

If someone is struggling to hear the voice of the Lord in some manner, you might suggest a break from sessions to go through a course of study with a mentor. Dr. Mark Virkler has an excellent book and study guide, *4 Keys to Hearing God's Voice.* See Appendix A for an article penned by Dr. Virkler on this subject.

*Scenario*: A person is not connecting with the way a question has been asked. Rather than moving on, take some time to ask the question several different ways.

I worked with a young man who continually challenged me to find different ways to ask the same question. He would sit in silence for a bit, pondering and listening. Then he would say something like, "I'm not getting it. Ask it another way." It was a great challenge, and we arrived at a connecting point with God as he responded to new ways of asking the same thing.

For instance, a facilitator might lead with this PAL, "Lord Jesus, I forgive _____ for sinning against me by (physically abusing me). I also choose to forgive _____ for the consequences of those actions. Lord, what are those consequences?" That does not connect for many participants. Other ways to ask are, "What do you think was stolen from you at that time in your life?" "What things have you missed out on as a result of _____'s actions against you?" "What things do you continue to miss out on?" "When you think about forgiving _____, about totally erasing their account with you, what do you think they still owe you? What things are still written on the ledger sheet waiting for an apology or restitution?" If the response is still "Nope, not getting it," put it this way, "What is the worst thing that could possibly happen if you let _____ off the hook for this sin against you?"

Notice I personalize the prayer/question with the person's name they are thinking about. This keeps the situation on a personal level rather than conceptual and enables their heart to deal with reality.

*Scenario*: The participant has shut down and nothing is happening. The ministry facilitator can sense they have gone "off duty."

Perhaps the prayer session has been intense, and the participant is drained emotionally and physically. It's probably wise to call it a day and set the time for the next session. You could PAL, "Lord Jesus, are we done for today?" Or, "Lord Jesus, I'm exhausted and having trouble staying engaged. Would it be okay to take a break now?" The Lord responds with words of comfort and encouragement as people pause and listen.

When nothing seems to be happening, you can pose these questions:

- Would you share what you are thinking right now?

- Would you share what you are feeling right now? Or, How are you feeling?

The participant might need to PAL, "Lord Jesus, I'm having a hard time staying focused and nothing seems to be happening. Can I just be with You for a while?"

Sit and listen, waiting for a connection. If nothing happens, it's okay to call it a day and try another time.

*Scenario*: The ministry facilitator gets off track from the "normal" sequence of the ministry plan and prayers.

You may think you have been taken through a maze in some sessions, following the lead of the Holy Spirit. Or perhaps you have followed a rabbit trail and are lost. What do you do?

It is always okay to take a time out. Say something like, "I need just a moment to gather my thoughts and ask the Lord where we are and what He wants to do right now." Then pray a prayer out loud, "Father, would you settle all of our hearts and give us direction for this moment? We need You to guide us."

Don't panic. Peace will settle in. Taking good notes during the session will help you track what has been covered and what is yet to be done. That's why you have a ministry plan in place to help guide you. Go back to where the prayer thread began and finish. Perhaps the participant realized they needed to forgive someone, and the conversation went to a word curse, ungodly thought pattern, or consequences. Following all of these areas needing prayer can be confusing if you aren't keeping track of what has been done and what still needs attention. Stay in peace and gently guide the participant in finishing the prayers for forgiveness and cleansing.

*Scenario*: What do you do when you are so frustrated or shocked you think thoughts you know you shouldn't say?

Intrigued? Read on.

# Liam's Story

Growing up for me was learning how to survive in one of the toughest neighborhoods in my area. Fighting to let off steam was a typical thing for teenage boys where I lived. Often I would get into fights in and out of school. Sometimes I got in trouble. However, after I gave my life to Jesus, I knew I needed to stop fighting. Yet I still craved the adrenaline-filled activity associated with violence – and as a result, felt a lot of guilt and shame.

One day in a SOULCARE ministry session with Carolyn Allen, I brought up this shame resulting from my unhealthy view of desiring to be "violent." I missed some of the adrenaline filled moments and became quite unhappy with my "mundane life." While taking out my frustration and anger about situations in my life with fistfights was no longer an option, I still experienced anger over the injustices in my life. Was I supposed to be silent about them?

## LORD, IN LIGHT OF WHAT I AM LEARNING, WHAT DOES THIS MEAN FOR ME IN MY LIFE?

Carolyn asked me to do some homework. I was to do a word study on the word "violence" and journal these questions: "Lord, in light of what I am learning, what does this mean for me in my life? Do I need to be afraid to be angry about injustice and to take a stand for what is right?"

I had never thought about asking a question like that before. The guilt and shame had blinded me to the truth that the Lord wanted to speak to me. Through the journaling exercise I learned about forgiveness and also about redemptive ways to express the intense emotions I still felt when injustices occurred. The strength of emotions (one of the definitions for the word violence) now moves me to speak up with the Lord's help. What is He saying, when is He saying it, and how is He saying it? These are now my guidelines when I feel an adrenaline rush and I need an outlet.

As I think of the times I get to be intensely passionate about the Gospel, confronting unrighteousness and trusting in the Lord to direct my conversations, I'm thankful that I no longer have to live as a slave to the incorrect definition of violence. Instead, I get to grow towards truth without the negativity hanging over my head and in my heart.

This completely different outlook of having a strength of emotion has changed my demeanor. My new mindset stops me from living in a shame-filled dialogue with myself and helps me look for Godly ways to express those powerful emotions. Violence expressed through fistfights and brawls that once produced shame is no longer an option for me. And speaking up and taking action with a new understanding of the word "violence" no longer produces guilt or shame.

Liam Graham

# CHAPTER TEN:

## *The "Don't Ask" Questions*

SOMEBODY SENT ME A CARTOON MEME THAT said, "Ask people questions that give them an opportunity to talk about themselves." The question posed was: "What the hell is wrong with you?"[18]

For some reason, I burst into laughter about this. I could identify with the question. There are just times we are so puzzled or frustrated about a person's situation that we find ourselves internally posing such questions. If we are drained physically or emotionally, it is easy to get frustrated. Or perhaps one of our own triggers gets pushed and we react rather than respond appropriately.

For example, one of my triggers is irrationality. When I think someone is being irrational, I have to remind myself we all think differently. I ask myself, "What is this person thinking that is causing them to emote and behave the way they are?" I might ask them, "Could you tell me what you are thinking and how you came to that conclusion?" This needs to be done respectfully, not in a condescending way, but with a desire to know what they think so I don't judge them. People always know if we are judging them. They can feel it.

Following are some of those questions that we might be thinking. We know we shouldn't say them, and hopefully we exercise the fruit of self-control before blurting them out and causing damage.

What is *wrong* with you?

Why are you acting like a *jerk*?

Don't you *know* what the Bible says to do?

Didn't you *think* about this before you did it?

Are you *kidding* me?

Have you thrown your *brains* on the floor?

Have you tried using your *head* for something besides a hat-rack lately?

You *what*?

Are you *stupid* or what?

Did *you* get up on the wrong side of the bed today or what?

Who tied *your* shoes for you this morning?

*Why* are you even here?

*What* are you doing?

Are you talking just to hear yourself talking? *What* is your point?

Why don't *you* put in some effort here and *do* something?

Right…not helpful! We know that!

But, what do we do when we find ourselves wanting to say something that we know will not be helpful? I have found it beneficial to recognize when I engage in former habit patterns of thoughts, feelings, and behaviors. We must know ourselves well and keep up to date as much as possible on our own journey into healing. Also, if I'm starting to show signs of being out of sorts, one of my colleagues is sure to let me know. We have given each other permission to speak this way into each others' lives. This is important! We all need accountability.

One day as I was praying with someone to help them on their journey of changing old habit patterns, the words *warning* and *weapon* dropped into my spirit. I heard the Lord say, "Ask them what their warning sign is when they are about to fall into an old way of thinking, feeling, or behaving. Ask them how they know when they are about to revert to an old default system. Then have them ask Me for a weapon to use against it."

## WE CHANGE THE WAY WE FEEL AND ACT BY CHANGING THE WAY WE THINK.

Applying this principle has proven to be helpful to me as well as many others. I PAL, "What feelings begin to arise within that let me know I will need to choose a new way of thinking?" Or, "What negative thought pattern will cause me to act in an unredemptive way?" In Romans 7:15 the Apostle Paul said, "Why do I do the things I don't want to do?" I believe we can pay attention to warning signs, whether they are particular thoughts that don't agree with God or old familiar feelings we have been trying to change. Sometimes we behave in a way we don't want, and that is also a warning. *We change the way we feel and act by changing the way we think.* Asking questions helps us stay on a path of discovery. We *can* choose a different path because "sin is no longer our master" (Romans 6:14). This is what I call "Yellow Light Theology."

Several years ago I was driving and approached a yellow stoplight. As I went through the yellow light without giving it a second thought, I heard the Holy Spirit say, "Carolyn, is that how you are going to respond to Me if I give you a caution about slowing or stopping when you are about to let your feelings control your behavior? What about when I am trying to teach you to stop and re-evaluate your perspective to change your responses? Are you going to keep right on moving?"

# I HAVE A CHOICE WHEN IT COMES TO MY THOUGHTS, FEELINGS AND BEHAVIOR.

In that moment, I realized that *I have a choice when it comes to my thoughts, feelings and behavior*. If I choose to go through the "yellow lights" instead of slowing or stopping, I will "do the things I don't want to do" and end up back in the cycle of defeating behaviors.

A warning sign is an opportunity to pause and PAL. Appendix F has a detailed *Warning & Weapon Activation* to help with this. We must continually pay attention to our warning signs and receive weapons from the Lord to use against them. Applying this skill is essential in all interactions, especially when we are facilitating healing in someone else's life.

Rather than verbalizing the random unkind thoughts we might have, let us always choose kindness. Let's let Jesus speak what He wants to through us. Jesus said He only did what He saw the Father doing and said what He heard the Father saying. He also listened for instructions to know when and how to carry out His assignments (John 5:19; 8:28-29). Let's allow Him to *be* the fruit of self-control through us in moments of frustration – it isn't worth the consequences if we ask the "Don't Ask" Questions.

When we choose kindness, we live the exchanged life on the journey of transformation! (Galatians 2:20)

# Cynthia's Story

God guides us in every aspect of our lives.

As a result of a series of events several years ago, my husband Bill and I realized the time had arrived for us to move from our condo in South Carolina. The first thing we did to respond to this challenge was ask this question: "Lord, what shall we do?"

Immediately I saw a picture of a broom in a sweeping motion, appearing to signal that sweeping changes were coming. Bill mentioned we might need to move back to Indiana where both of us had previously lived.

As we continued to seek the Lord, I had a dream that showed a map of the United States. Indiana stood out as it was a deep velvet purple, and the other states were beige. I also heard the Don Moen song "God Will Make a Way Where There Seems to be No Way."

We pressed into God, asking, "How will we know when the answer is from you, Lord?" We got the idea that if we did not force the selling of the condo, it would help us know if we were going in the right direction. We did not list it but just told prayer partners.

Almost immediately an offer came. However, when we prayed about this offer. I saw a picture of the Muckraker from Pilgrim's Progress (whose eyes were fixed on carnal things, not spiritual). We knew this financial offer wasn't the right one.

The second offer we received turned out to be perfect for us.

In every home the realtor showed us, we prayed for wisdom. "Lord, is this the one for us?" The one we both liked was just the size we needed, and we wouldn't even need a mortgage.

Before we came to Fort Wayne, we prayed and asked where our home church would be. I had a vision of a Native American on his horse pulling a travois indicating "Midwest or Heartland." We wanted to be a part of an Anglican church, so our priest prayed we would find one. The only one we found was "Heartland Church." We connected immediately with the leadership and congregation.

God led us each step of the way as we continually asked for His guidance. We didn't receive the whole picture with the first question; we continued asking until we were directed where to position ourselves for the next season of our lives. And God was faithful to answer!

Cynthia Thompson

# CHAPTER ELEVEN:

## *Keys to Frame Questions*

"I AM SUCH A DISASTER. I AM SO STUPID I CAN'T do anything right as a parent. I have messed up so many times my children will never get over it. I am responsible for it all. I made this happen. My son is expelled from school and is in the detention center. He is angry and won't talk to me. My other two children are acting out. They aren't sleeping and they fight all the time. I am angry, tired and anxious. I cry a lot and can't even think straight. What is wrong with me? Why did I even become a parent?"

The discouragement, fatigue and hopelessness in the room were tangible. I could almost reach out and touch them. I could empathize, but how could I help this person engage with the Lord?

At this point, my inner dialogue with God went something like this: "What is the best question to have this person ask You for them to change their path? What will give them hope?"

YOU CAN'T FIX ANYONE'S PROBLEMS, YOU ARE NOT THEIR POWER SOURCE, AND YOU ARE NOT RESPONSIBLE FOR THEIR HEALING.

Taking a moment to PAL (Pause, Ask and Listen) for yourself may seem like a waste of time when you want to jump right in and offer a solution to fix the problem. This is the time to remember that you can't fix anyone's problems, you are not their power source, and you are not responsible for their healing. This moment is ripe for the opportunity to put your conversation on the right trajectory. A well-crafted question helps open the door to discovery.

## PAL: PAUSE, ASK, LISTEN

While using PAL in this context, these guidelines will help you:

- Pause: Take a deep breath. Becoming nervous diminishes your ability to think clearly. Do your best to stay calm. The Holy Spirit is helping you. Have a declaration that will encourage and support you.[19] I use this statement regularly: "Lord Jesus, because You are at my right hand, I will not be shaken" (Psalm 16:8).

- Ask: "Lord, what question will help this person at this moment?" or "Lord, what do You want me to ask?"

- Listen: Take time to listen to the Lord. He is full of wisdom and gives it generously to those who ask (James 1:5).

A central issue underlies the person's helplessness and frustration in the shared illustration. What words have they been using to describe their thoughts, feelings and behavior? Using their words helps them identify with the conversation you want them to start with God.

The questions you pose will also be more effective when you use their language because they are already in that space. Listen carefully. Write down their key words as they talk to help you remember them. Listen dually. By that, I mean listen to the Holy Spirit leading and directing you as you listen to the person in front of you. Listen heart to heart and head to head to what they are saying. The more you practice this skill, the more you will hear the 'feeling' words and the thoughts stirring the feelings. Listen empathically – beyond what they say – to feel what they feel and why.

When you have accurately discerned someone's thoughts and feelings, put yourself in their position. Think their thoughts and feel their feelings. Ask yourself, "What questions will help me gain a new perspective so that I can move from this space of negativity and condemnation to a path of discovery and hope?" Then shift from identifying with the participant to functioning as a ministry facilitator. Initiate a dialogue between them and God. This process might seem long or tedious, but the more you exercise the technique, the more you will find yourself moving into and out of this position in moments.

After asking a discovery question, listen carefully to the response. As facilitators, we aren't looking to blame people or judge them. We aren't looking to impress them with our knowledge or expertise. We desire to help them hear Jesus speak what is necessary for healing and rest in their soul and body.

Here are some key concepts to use when framing a discovery question:

- What is the purpose of this question? Does it address the issue?

- Will this question lead to a conversation with me or be an invitation to a conversation with Jesus?

- Will this question cloud the person's mind with negativity about God's character? Of their character? Or will it stretch their holy imagination about a new way to think and walk in the Spirit?

- Is this question present-future oriented? Will it draw the person closer to God and where He wants to take them?

- Will this question evoke a response that is self-condemning or God-focused?

- Is this question invitational rather than confrontational?

Even if confrontation (i.e., pointing out inconsistencies) is necessary, the interchange can still be an invitation. It can be solution-oriented versus blame-oriented.

Avoid using "why" questions such as, "Why did you do/say that?" "Why" questions tend to be accusatory, put people on the defensive, and hinder their ability to think clearly.

Instead, ask "what/how" questions. "What/how" questions activate thinking and participation. The person is empowered to be an overcomer rather than a victim.

Following are some helpful "what/how" questions:

What prompted you to say/do that?

What result were you hoping for?

What result did you get?

What can you do or say differently next time that will facilitate reaching your goal?

What would change about your behavior if you chose a different thought about this?

## INVITATIONS TO SOLUTIONS KEEP THE CONVERSATION ISSUE-FOCUSED RATHER THAN PERSONALITY-FOCUSED.

Invitations to solutions keep the conversation issue-focused rather than personality-focused. Instead of "Why are you this way?" ask, "What is the issue? What is a different way you can think in order to reach a redemptive solution?"

*Change your thoughts, change your life.*
*Change your questions, change your life.*

## LEARNING TO CHANGE OUR INNER DIALOGUE/ QUESTIONS AS SOON AS A PATTERN IS RECOGNIZED IS A KEY TO TRANSFORMATION.

Since most of our inner dialogue is question-based and reflects habit patterns, we often revert to behaviors stemming from legalism. We end up in negativity and condemnation when discovery and new paths are available to us. *Learning to change our inner dialogue/questions as soon as a pattern is recognized is a key to transformation.*

Discovery questions lay the Scriptural foundations that God is present, God speaks to His children today, and God can be understood and obeyed.

An excellent transitional question to refocus the attention to Jesus is: "Wow _____, you are dealing with a lot right now. How about we ask Jesus a question and see what He has to say about all you are going through?" Using their words, form a question and start a conversation with the Lord:

Their words: "Lord Jesus, I am such a disaster. I think I am so stupid that I can't do anything right as a parent. I have messed up so many times my children will never get over it, and I am responsible for it."

Following are some possible ministry questions to help the person move from condemnation to discovery with the Holy Spirit. Have them ask the Lord and listen for a response.

- "Lord, I am ready to take responsibility for the things I have done wrong as a parent. What would You like to say to me about this?" LISTEN.

- "Lord, are there things You would like me to ask forgiveness for?" LISTEN.

- "Lord, would you please forgive me?" LISTEN.

- "Lord, I feel _____ (worthless, ashamed, guilty, or responsible) because I think _____. This kind of thinking is causing me to _____ (behavior – be depressed, withdraw from family and friends). I don't want to live this way anymore. Is it true my kids will never get over what I've done?" LISTEN.

- "Lord, have I messed up too many times?" LISTEN.

- "Lord, am I a disaster? Stupid?" LISTEN.

- "Lord, is it true I can't do anything right as a parent?" LISTEN.

- "Lord, since the questions I have been asking are empowering negative thinking and ungodly behavior, I want to know what Your thoughts are. I want different fruit in my life. What are You thinking about this right now? What do You want me to think about this? I want to agree with You." LISTEN.

To reinforce what the Lord speaks to the participant as they listen have them PAL this:

"Lord, the next time I face a situation and think I'm a terrible parent, with Your help I will think _____. How will this new way of thinking affect my behavior?" This PAL enables the participant to use their new weapon (new thought from the Lord) and warning (in this case, an ungodly way of thinking). (See chapter ten and Appendices E and F.)

The questions that start with "Why am I so…," can be challenged and changed as we ask the Holy Spirit, "What is a better question to ask?" Asking the right questions at the right time helps people:

- think more clearly and focus

- take responsibility for themselves

- accomplish their goals

- discover truth and direction

- engage in conversation and relationships more effectively

- think about consequences

- maneuver change

- realize that the healing journey is process-driven versus a quick fix

- discover the keys to transformation

- direct their attention, perception, energy, and effort

- move to action and change their behavior

- think solution-oriented versus problem-oriented

- learn versus judge and condemn themselves and others

- discern inner self-talk that leads to feelings and behaviors

- structure what they want to say and therefore do

If we ask the wrong questions, we get the wrong answers. If we ask the right questions of the Right Person, we will get the right answers to solve our challenges. As you frame questions, be thoughtful and choose wisely to empower a fruitful life.

# Your Story

You have read how questions can influence thinking that either leads to a path of discovery or to a path that is condemning and shaming. You have seen how redemptive questions facilitate a positive change of direction in the lives of people who shared their God stories.

I encourage you to take time to write your own story of how God is using or has used the concepts presented in *Life-Changing Questions* in your life. What would your story be? Spend time thinking about how asking a question a different way has changed your life. Or consider how a question is currently being used by God or others to cause you to think differently.

Write your story and share it with others to encourage them on their journey.

# CONCLUSION

WE HAVE EXPLORED MANY FACETS OF THE BOLD statement that *Questions determine the course of our lives*. We have discovered the importance of asking questions on our journey, how we ask them and who we ask. Are our questions taking us on a path of discovery with the Holy Spirit or a path of self-condemnation, guilt and shame?

Since we all ask both kinds of questions, the key is to remember that we get to choose which kinds to ask. We are continuously choosing what to think by asking the right question to the Right Person. Choosing to habituate ourselves in a new way of thinking is crucial to our transformation. A question asked at the right time can alter our perspective of any circumstance and change our course of direction. Powerful questions shift our thinking and the behaviors that follow.

POWERFUL QUESTIONS SHIFT OUR THINKING
AND THE BEHAVIORS THAT FOLLOW.

If I could choose my "top ten" questions that could apply to almost any everyday situation, this would be my list:

10. Lord, is the expectation I have of (You, others, myself) realistic?

9. Lord, I'm not getting the results I want by asking this question (_____). What is a better question to ask?

8. Lord, what is my responsibility in this situation?

7. Lord, what assumptions am I making about this person/situation?

   When You think about _____, what do You think?

6. Lord, what are You teaching me (from this person/situation/failure/success)?

5. Lord, I'm thinking this _____. Is this okay with You?

4. What thought is resulting in this ungodly behavior?

   What thought will result in a Godly behavior?

   If I adopt this Godly thought, how will my behavior change?

   Fill in the blank: When I think _____, I feel _____. Then I _____.

3. What thought is producing this negatively expressed emotion? (i.e. angry, impatient, confused, helpless, hopeless, stingy)

   What thought will produce a Kingdom of God emotion? (i.e. loving, safe, peaceful, gentle, strong, generous)

   Fill in the blank: When I think _____, I feel _____.

2. Lord, who do You want to be for me right now?

1. Lord, is there another way for me to look at or think about this situation/person?

# WHAT HOLDS YOU STEADY WHEN EVERYTHING ABOUT YOU IS SHAKING?

I offer one last question for you to consider. What holds you steady when everything about you is shaking, when you get discouraged and want to quit, or when you wonder if there is even a good reason to do what you are doing? We have all had those feelings, and we all need encouragement. Otherwise, there is a potential to make a choice we could later regret.

A verse or passage of Scripture can hold us steady. I call this a "life verse" or "life passage." When I read Colossians 1, I get tears in my eyes, and my heart softens – even during a discouraging, trying season. It always reminds me of my purpose and that Jesus is the one supplying the energy I need. I like the way the Message frames this in contemporary language: "We preach Christ, warning people not to add to the Message. We teach in a spirit of profound common sense so that we can bring each person to maturity. To be mature is to be basic. Christ! No more, no less. That's what I'm working so hard at day after day, year after year, doing my best with the energy God so generously gives me" (Colossians 1:28-29 MSG).

Do you have a life verse or passage? If not, ask the Lord (PAL), "Lord, what verse or passage of Scripture do You want me to embrace as encouragement when I am tired, frustrated, discouraged, and tempted to quit?"

Spend some time listening and journaling until you find affirming reassurance in His Word. I can't emphasize strongly enough how life-changing this question and the answer you hear will be.

Perhaps you will have several passages of Scripture like this. I do. Every time I read or think about them, I experience His presence and peace. I am humbled as I remember that He cares all the time about what I am going through, and He never leaves me on my own.

Practice the skill of asking questions as you refocus your daily inner dialogue. Practice with your family and co-workers. Listen, listen, listen – to God and people – and you will be amazed at how new doors of possibilities open for you. You will soon find yourself on a path of discovery with the Holy Spirit.

Asking great questions can *change the course of your life!*

ASKING GREAT QUESTIONS CAN CHANGE THE
COURSE OF YOUR LIFE!

# APPENDICES
# A THROUGH F

# APPENDIX A:

## *"How to Hear God's Voice"*

**Dr. Mark Virkler (used by permission)**

She had done it again! Instead of coming straight home from school like she was supposed to, she had gone to her friend's house. Without permission. Without our knowledge. Without doing her chores.

With a ministering household that included remnants of three struggling families plus our own toddler and newborn, my wife simply couldn't handle all the work on her own. Everyone had to pull their own weight. Everyone had age-appropriate tasks they were expected to complete. At fourteen, Rachel and her younger brother were living with us while her parents tried to overcome lifestyle patterns that had resulted in the children running away to escape the dysfunction. I felt sorry for Rachel, but, honestly my wife was my greatest concern. Now Rachel had ditched her chores to spend time with her friends. It wasn't the first time, but if I had anything to say about it, it would be the last. I intended to lay down the law when she got home and make it very clear that if she was going to live under my roof, she would obey my rules.

But…she wasn't home yet. And I had recently been learning to hear God's voice more clearly. Maybe I should try to see if I could hear anything from Him about the situation. Maybe He could give me a way to get her to do what she was supposed to (i.e., what I wanted her to do). So I went to my office and reviewed what the Lord had been teaching me from Habakkuk 2:1,2: "I will stand on my guard post and station myself on the rampart; And I will keep watch to see what He will speak to me…Then the Lord answered me and said, 'Record the vision….'"

Habakkuk said, "I will stand on my guard post..." (Habakkuk 2:1). **The first key to hearing God's voice is to go to a quiet place and still our own thoughts and emotions.** Psalm 46:10 encourages us to be still, let go, cease striving, and know that He is God. In Psalm 37:7 we are called to "be still before the Lord and wait patiently for Him." There is a deep inner knowing in our spirits that each of us can experience when we quiet our flesh and our minds. Practicing the art of biblical meditation helps silence the outer noise and distractions clamoring for our attention.

I didn't have a guard post but I did have an office, so I went there to quiet my temper and my mind. Loving God through a quiet worship song is one very effective way to become still. In 2 Kings 3, Elisha needed a word from the Lord so he said, "Bring me a minstrel," and as the minstrel played, the Lord spoke. I have found that playing a worship song on my autoharp is the quickest way for me to come to stillness. I need to choose my song carefully; boisterous songs of praise do not bring me to stillness, but rather gentle songs that express my love and worship. And it isn't enough just to sing the song into the cosmos – I come into the Lord's presence most quickly and easily when I use my godly imagination to see the truth that He is right here with me and I sing my songs to Him, personally.

"I will keep watch to see," said the prophet. To receive the pure word of God, it is very important that my heart be properly focused as I become still, because my focus is the source of the intuitive flow. If I fix my eyes upon Jesus (Hebrews 12:2), the intuitive flow comes from Jesus. But if I fix my gaze upon some desire of my heart, the intuitive flow comes out of that desire. To have a pure flow I must become still and carefully fix my eyes upon Jesus. Quietly worshiping the King and receiving out of the stillness that follows quite easily accomplishes this. So I used **the second key to hearing God's voice: As you pray, fix the eyes of your heart upon Jesus, seeing in the**

**Spirit the dreams and visions of Almighty God.** Habakkuk was actually looking for vision as he prayed. He opened the eyes of his heart, and looked into the spirit world to see what God wanted to show him.

God has always spoken through dreams and visions, and He specifically said that they would come to those upon whom the Holy Spirit is poured out (Acts 2:1-4, 17). Being a logical, rational person, observable facts that could be verified by my physical senses were the foundations of my life, including my spiritual life. I had never thought of opening the eyes of my heart and looking for vision. However, I have come to believe that this is exactly what God wants me to do. He gave me eyes in my heart to see in the spirit the vision and movement of Almighty God. There is an active spirit world all around us, full of angels, demons, the Holy Spirit, the omnipresent Father, and His omnipresent Son, Jesus. The only reasons for me not to see this reality are unbelief or lack of knowledge.

In his sermon in Acts 2:25, Peter refers to King David's statement: "I saw the Lord always in my presence; for He is at my right hand, so that I will not be shaken." The original psalm makes it clear that this was a decision of David's, not a constant supernatural visitation: "I have set (literally, I have placed) the Lord continually before me; because He is at my right hand, I will not be shaken" (Psalm 16:8). Because David knew that the Lord was always with him, he determined in his spirit to *see* that truth with the eyes of his heart as he went through life, knowing that this would keep his faith strong.

In order to see, we must look. Daniel saw a vision in his mind and said, "I was looking...I kept looking...I kept looking" (Daniel 7:2, 9, 13). As I pray, I look for Jesus, and I watch as He speaks to me, doing and saying the things that are on His heart. Many Christians will find that if they only look, they will see. Jesus is Emmanuel, God with us (Matthew 1:23). It is as simple as that. You can see Christ present with you because Christ *is* present with you. In fact, the vision may come so easily that you will be tempted to reject it, thinking that it is just you. But if you persist in recording these visions, your doubt will soon be overcome by faith as you recognize that the content of them could only be birthed in Almighty God.

Jesus demonstrated the ability of living out of constant contact with God, declaring that He did nothing on His own initiative, but only what He saw the Father doing, and heard the Father saying (John 5:19,20,30). What an incredible way to live! Is it possible for us to live out of divine initiative as Jesus did? Yes! We must simply fix our eyes upon Jesus. The veil has been torn, giving access into the immediate presence of God, and He calls us to draw near (Luke 23:45; Hebrews 10:19-22). "I pray that the eyes of your heart will be enlightened…."

When I had quieted my heart enough that I was able to picture Jesus without the distractions of my own ideas and plans, I was able to "keep watch to see what He will speak to me." I wrote down my question: "Lord, what should I do about Rachel?" Immediately the thought came to me, "She is insecure." Well, that certainly wasn't my thought! Her behavior looked like rebellion to me, not insecurity.

But like Habakkuk, I was coming to know the sound of God speaking to me (Habakkuk 2:2). Elijah described it as a still, small voice (I Kings 19:12). I had previously listened for an inner audible voice, and God does speak that way at times. However, I have found that usually, God's voice comes as spontaneous thoughts, visions, feelings, or impressions.

For example, haven't you been driving down the road and had a thought come to you to pray for a certain person? Didn't you believe it was God telling you to pray? What did God's voice sound like? Was it an audible voice, or was it a spontaneous thought that lit upon your mind?

Experience indicates that we perceive spirit-level communication as spontaneous thoughts, impressions and visions, and Scripture confirms this in many ways. For example, one definition of *paga*, a Hebrew word for intercession, is "a chance encounter or an accidental intersecting." When God lays people on our hearts, He does it through *paga*, a chance-encounter thought "accidentally" intersecting our minds.

So **the third key to hearing God's voice is recognizing that God's voice in your heart often sounds like a flow of spontaneous thoughts.** Therefore, when I want to hear from God, I tune to chance-encounter or spontaneous thoughts.

Finally, God told Habakkuk to record the vision (Habakkuk 2:2). This was not an isolated command. The Scriptures record many examples of individual's prayers and God's replies, such as the Psalms, many of the prophets, and Revelation. I have found that obeying this final principle amplified my confidence in my ability to hear God's voice so that I could finally make living out of His initiatives a way of life. The **fourth key, two-way journaling or the writing out of your prayers and God's answers, brings great freedom in hearing God's voice.**

I have found two-way journaling to be a fabulous catalyst for clearly discerning God's inner, spontaneous flow, because as I journal I am able to write in faith for long periods of time, simply believing it is God. I know that what I believe I have received from God must be tested. However, testing involves doubt and doubt blocks divine communication, so I do not want to test while I am trying to receive. (See James 1:5-8.) With journaling, I can receive in faith, knowing that when the flow has ended I can test and examine it carefully.

So I wrote down what I believed He had said: "She is insecure." But the Lord wasn't done. I continued to write the spontaneous thoughts that came to me: "Love her unconditionally. She is flesh of your flesh and bone of your bone." My mind immediately objected: She is not flesh of my flesh. She is not related to me at all – she is a foster child, just living in my home temporarily. It was definitely time to test this "word from the Lord"!

There are three possible sources of thoughts in our minds: ourselves, satan and the Holy Spirit. It was obvious that the words in my journal did not come from my own mind – I certainly didn't see her as insecure *or* flesh of my flesh. And I sincerely doubted that satan would encourage me to love anyone unconditionally!

Okay, it was starting to look like I might have actually received counsel from the Lord. It was consistent with the names and character of God as revealed in the Scripture, and totally contrary to the names and character of the enemy. So that meant that I was hearing from the Lord, and He wanted me to see the situation in a different light. Rachel was my daughter – part of my family not by blood but by the hand of God Himself. The chaos of her birth home had created deep insecurity about her worthiness to be loved by anyone, including me and including God. Only the unconditional love of the Lord expressed through an imperfect human would reach her heart.

But there was still one more test I needed to perform before I would have absolute confidence that this was truly God's word to me: I needed confirmation from someone else whose spiritual discernment I trusted. So I went to my wife and shared what I had received. I knew if I could get her validation, especially since she was the one most wronged in the situation, then I could say, at least to myself, "Thus sayeth the Lord."

Needless to say, Patti immediately and without question confirmed that the Lord had spoken to me. My entire planned lecture was forgotten. I returned to my office anxious to hear more. As the Lord planted a new, supernatural love for Rachel within me, He showed me what to say and how to say it to not only address the current issue of household responsibility, but the deeper issues of love and acceptance and worthiness.

Rachel and her brother remained as part of our family for another two years, giving us many opportunities to demonstrate and teach about the Father's love, planting spiritual seeds in thirsty soil. We weren't perfect and we didn't solve all of her issues, but because I had learned to listen to the Lord, we were able to avoid creating more brokenness and separation.

The four simple keys that the Lord showed me from Habakkuk have been used by people of all ages, from four to a hundred and four, from every continent, culture and denomination, to break through into intimate two-way conversations with their loving Father and dearest Friend. Omitting any one of the keys will prevent you from receiving all He wants to say to you. The order of the keys is not important, just that you *use them all*. Embracing all four, by faith, can change your life. Simply quiet yourself down, tune to spontaneity, look for vision, and journal. He is waiting to meet you there.

You will be amazed when you journal! Doubt may hinder you at first, but throw it off, reminding yourself that it is a biblical concept, and that God is present, speaking to His children. Relax. When we cease our labors and enter His rest, God is free to flow (Hebrews 4:10).

Why not try it for yourself, right now? Sit back comfortably, take out your pen and paper, and smile. Turn your attention toward the Lord in praise and worship, seeking His face. Many people have found the music and visionary prayer called "A Stroll Along the Sea of Galilee" helpful in getting them started. You can listen to it and download it free at www.CWGMinistries.org/Galilee.

After you write your question to Him, become still, fixing your gaze on Jesus. You will suddenly have a very good thought. Don't doubt it; simply write it down. Later, as you read your journaling, you, too, will be blessed to discover that you are indeed dialoguing with God. If you wonder if it is really the Lord speaking to you, share it with your spouse or a friend. Their input will encourage your faith and strengthen your commitment to spend time getting to know the Lover of your soul more intimately than you ever dreamed possible.

### Is It *Really* God?

Five ways to be sure what you're hearing is from Him:

### 1. Test the Origin (1 John 4:1)

Thoughts from our own minds are progressive, with one thought leading to the next, however tangentially. Thoughts from the spirit world are spontaneous. The Hebrew word for true prophecy is *naba*, which literally means to bubble up, whereas false prophecy is *ziyd* meaning to boil up. True words from the Lord will bubble up from our innermost being; we don't need to cook them up ourselves.

### 2. Compare It to Biblical Principles

God will never say something to you personally which is contrary to His universal revelation as expressed in the Scriptures. If the Bible clearly states that something is a sin, no amount of journaling can make it right. Much of what you journal about will not be specifically addressed in the Bible, however, so an understanding of biblical principles is also needed.

### 3. Compare It to the Names and Character of God as Revealed in the Bible

Anything God says to you will be in harmony with His essential nature. Journaling will help you get to *know* God personally, but knowing what the Bible says *about* Him will help you discern what words are from Him. Make sure the tenor of your journaling lines up with the character of God as described in the names of the Father, Son and Holy Spirit.

### 4. Test the Fruit (Matthew 7:15-20)

What effect does what you are hearing have on your soul and your spirit? Words from the Lord will quicken your faith and increase your love, peace and joy. They will stimulate a sense of humility within you as you become more aware of Who God is and who you are. On the other hand, any words you receive which cause you to fear or doubt, which bring you into confusion or anxiety, or which stroke your ego (especially if you hear something that is "just for you alone – no one else is worthy") must be immediately rebuked and rejected as lies of the enemy.

### 5. Share It with Your Spiritual Counselors (Proverbs 11:14)

We are members of a Body! A cord of three strands is not easily broken and God's intention has always been for us to grow together. Nothing will increase your faith in your ability to hear from God like having it confirmed by two or three other people! Share it with your spouse, your parents, your friends, your elder, your group leader, even your grown children can be your sounding board. They don't need to be perfect or super-spiritual; they just need to love you, be committed to being available to you, have a solid biblical orientation, and most importantly, they must also willingly and easily receive counsel. Avoid the authoritarian who insists that because of their standing in the church or with God, they no longer need to listen to others. Find two or three people and let them confirm that you are hearing from God!

The book *4 Keys to Hearing God's Voice* is available at www. CWGMinistries.org.

## Introduction to Appendices B through D

Appendices B through D are for you to use for an interactive dialogue experience with the Lord.

Paraphrasing is one way to help you meditate on Scripture and habituate your thoughts. When you paraphrase, you can look up key words in the dictionary or Strong's Concordance to impart a new personal meaning to the Word.

For example: "And do not be conformed to this world, but be transformed by the renewing of your mind" (Romans 12:2a). Carolyn's paraphrase: "Carolyn, don't accommodate yourself to the ways of the world. Don't get caught up trying to be like everyone else. It is better for you to activate your mind to agree with Jesus Christ so you can become like Jesus in character and conduct."

Spend some of your devotional time with God to let the truth of these Scriptures sink into your heart. When we PAL – Pause, Ask, Listen – with the Lord, we are using the principles of Lectio Divina (Latin for "Divine Reading"), an ancient way of reading the Bible. It allows for and trains the participant in a quiet and contemplative way of approaching God's Word. This method of engaging with the Holy Spirit and Scripture will deepen your intimacy with Him.

The main elements in Lectio Divina are:

- Choose a passage of Scripture.

- Find a place of stillness before God.

- Read the section of Scripture two times, slowly. Let the words sink into your heart. Meditate on what you have heard. If a word or phrase stands out to you, write it down.

- Reread the passage two times.

- What are you hearing? What are you feeling? Write it down.

- Does this passage bring to mind any particular memories or experiences?

- Write these down.

- *PAL: "Holy Spirit, what do You want to say to me about these experiences?*

- Read the passage a final two times.

- Meditate on it. Be still and let the words minister to you.

- *PAL: "God, is there something You want me to do in response to this passage?"*

- Write it down.

- *PAL: "God, what do You want me to think in light of what you have been saying to me from this passage?"*

- Write down His thoughts and your conversation with Him.

Appendix B, *Jesus Questions Devotions*, is based on a few of Jesus' questions. Using Lectio Divina guidelines, read the noted passage of Scripture and do the activations. There are specific questions for you to PAL. If you enjoy these activations and would like to do more, you can find a list of some of the questions Jesus asked in the gospels at this website:

https://blog.adw.org/wp-content/uploads/2015/08/100-Questions-that-Jesus-asked-and-YOU-must-answer.pdf

You can also use the principles of Lecto Divinia to engage with the truths of *Christ in Me Is...*and *In Christ I am...*in Appendices C and D.

Be sure to test your journaling with these guidelines from Mark Virkler that were presented in chapter one.

1. Test the origin (1 John 4:1).

2. Compare it to biblical principles.

3. Compare it to the names and character of God as revealed in the Bible.

4. Test the Fruit (Matthew 7:15-20).

5. Share it with your spiritual counselors (Proverbs 11:14).

Be blessed, encouraged and challenged as you interact with Jesus – the One who modeled asking questions in so many of His encounters with people.

# APPENDIX B:

## *Introduction to Jesus Questions Devotions*

This appendix is based on a few of the questions Jesus asked in the gospels and is designed for you to use as an interactive dialogue experience with the Lord. Use this at your own pace and enjoy taking time to PAL – Pause, Ask, Listen – with the Lord. Use the principles of Lectio Divina as explained in the introduction to Appendices B through D.

Find a quiet place, read the question with surrounding verses a few times, allowing the words to sink into your heart. What is standing out to you? How are your emotions responding to the question? What are you seeing, hearing and feeling? Write this down.

Keep rereading the passage of Scripture.

Does the passage, or particularly the question, bring to mind any particular memories or experiences? Write these down.

PAL: "Holy Spirit, what do You want to say to me about these experiences?"

Be sure to test your journaling with the guidelines from Mark Virkler.

With each passage of Scripture, there are specific questions for you to PAL. In addition, here are some general questions you can also use:

What opportunity does this question give me to embrace a truth?

How does this apply to me in my life right now?

"Lord Jesus, would You cause the truth of what You were saying (to the disciples, the Pharisees, etc.) to penetrate my heart so I can be more like You?"

You're next...enjoy your encounters with Jesus.

## "Who Do You Say That I Am?"

*Now, when Jesus came into the district of Caesarea Philippi, He was asking His disciples, "Who do people say that the Son of Man is?" And they said, "Some say John the Baptist; and others, Elijah; but still others, Jeremiah, or one of the prophets." He said to them, "But **who do you say that I am?**" Simon Peter answered, "You are the Christ, the Son of the living God." And Jesus said to him, "Blessed are you, Simon Barjona, because flesh and blood did not reveal this to you, but My Father who is in Heaven* (Matthew 16:13-17).

Can you hear Jesus saying to you today, "Who do you say I am? Who am I to you?" How would you answer Him? Think of a situation you are in, perhaps a relationship or a challenge at work, or a parenting dilemma. Think in a big picture about who He is to you, then ask Him, "Who do You want to be for me in this situation?"

PAL: Answer Jesus' question: "Who do you say I am?"

PAL: Jesus, who do You want to be for me in this specific situation? (i.e. healer, teacher, truth, faithfulness, encourager, peace, etc.)

What will this look like in my life?

How will knowing and embracing this truth change my behavior?

### PRAYER

"Lord Jesus, I thank You for being who You are to and for me. Today, You have spoken to my heart and said You are _____ to me. When I think about You in this way, I feel _____ and want to love You more deeply. I want to know everything I can about You. I love you."

### DECLARATION

Jesus, today I am choosing to see You as _____ and, with Your help, will endeavor to live my life based on this reality. With Your help I will let You be _____ through me.

### "What Do You Want Me To Do For You?"

*Then they came to Jericho. And as He was leaving Jericho with His disciples and a large crowd, a blind beggar named Bartimaeus, the son of Timaeus, was sitting by the road. When he heard that it was Jesus the Nazarene, he began to cry out and say, "Jesus, Son of David, have mercy on me!" Many were sternly telling him to be quiet, but he kept crying out all the more, "Son of David, have mercy on me!" And Jesus stopped and said, "Call him here." So they called the blind man, saying to him, "Take courage, stand up! He is calling for you." Throwing aside his cloak, he jumped up and came to Jesus. And answering him, Jesus said, "What do you want Me to do for you?" And the blind man said to Him, "Rabboni, I want to regain my sight!" And Jesus said to him, "Go; your faith has made you well." Immediately he regained his sight and began following Him on the road"( Mark 10:46-52).*

Has your desperation ever brought you to a place where you kept asking and asking and asking for Jesus to have mercy on you and answer your request? Can you put yourself in this story and, using your holy imagination, picture Jesus coming to you in response to your persistence and asking, "What do you want Me to do for you?"

Today, how would you answer that question? What do you want Jesus to do for you today?

Let's PAL: "Jesus, today I need _____. Is it okay for me to ask You for _____? What would You like to say to me about this right now?"

Journal what you see, hear, and feel.

PAL: "Lord Jesus is there a Scripture You would like me to read that will help me regarding this issue?"

PAL: "Lord Jesus, is there some action You want me to take regarding this?"

## PRAYER

"Lord Jesus, thank You that I can come to You with every need I have. Thank You for listening, caring, and speaking Your wisdom and truth to me. Your words are life to me. Your precious Name tastes like honey in my mouth. I love You, Jesus."

## DECLARATION

Jesus, with Your help, I choose to take the action You revealed to Me today. I will rely on Your strength and wisdom as I obey You step by step. I trust You to live Your life through me to do what You want to do. I have confidence You will empower me to complete what I start.

## "What Good Is It To Gain The Whole World And Forfeit His Soul?"

*And He summoned the crowd with His disciples, and said to them, "If anyone wishes to come after Me, he must deny himself, and take up his cross and follow Me. For whoever wishes to save his life will lose it, but whoever loses his life for My sake and the gospel's will save it. **For what does it profit a man to gain the whole world, and forfeit his soul? For what will a man give in exchange for his soul?** For whoever is ashamed of Me and My words in this adulterous and sinful generation, the Son of Man will also be ashamed of him when He comes in the glory of His Father with the holy angels* (Mark 8:34-38).

"What does it profit a man to gain the whole world, and forfeit his soul?" The answer is implied within the question. What is the implication?

PAL: "Lord Jesus, is there an area in my heart where I have compromised to gain something the world offers, and my soul is hurting and neglected because of it?" (Some areas to look at might be position, power, security, performance, perfectionism – anything you are pursuing that takes the place of God.)

PAL: "Have I tried to exchange Your best for something I want instead?" Journal what you see, hear, and feel.

PAL: "Lord Jesus, what are You saying to me as I read this Scripture today and hear You asking me, '_____ (your name), what will you gain if you keep this place in your heart withheld from me? I have a better way for you.'"

### PRAYER

"Lord Jesus, I pray this with the psalmist, "Search me, O God, and know my heart; test me and know my anxious thoughts. Point out anything in me that offends You, and lead me along the path of everlasting life" (Psalms 139:23-24 NLT).

## DECLARATION

Jesus, I declare that You are worth more to me than _____. I am not ashamed of You and Your gospel. With the help of the Holy Spirit, I will learn what it means to submit my desires to Your will. I want to be fully available to You.

## "Why Are You Troubled, and Why Do Doubts Rise in Your Hearts?"

*While they were telling these things, He Himself stood in their midst and said to them, "Peace be to you." But they were startled and frightened and thought that they were seeing a spirit. And He said to them, "**Why are you troubled, and why do doubts arise in your hearts?** See My hands and My feet, that it is I Myself; touch Me and see, for a spirit does not have flesh and bones as you see that I have." And when He had said this, He showed them His hands and His feet. While they still could not believe it because of their joy and amazement, He said to them, "Have you anything here to eat?" They gave Him a piece of a broiled fish; and He took it and ate it before them* (Luke 24:36-43).

There are times in our lives when we struggle with doubts and fears, even when Jesus has spoken, "Peace be to you." Sometimes we need to see and hear something more to alleviate our doubts. Jesus took a step beyond speaking those words to the disciples when He showed them physical evidence of the wounds on His hands and feet as if He were saying, "Yes, this is really me and here is the evidence." When they still could not believe it, He took yet another step and asked them to eat with Him.

Jesus really wants us to live in the provision of His Presence that is Peace in the midst of our doubts and fears. He is patient with us as we ask our questions and arrive at a place of rest in Him – even in the most serious of situations.

Are you experiencing doubt in some situation in your life? How would you answer this question Jesus asked? PAL: "_____ (your name), why are you troubled, and why do doubts arise in your heart?" What thoughts would you share with Him?

PAL: "Jesus, what would You like to say to me about these doubts and struggles I have?"

PAL: "Jesus, what is my place to stand as I work through this?"

Listen and journal what you see, hear and feel.

**PRAYER**

"Lord Jesus, even when I'm doubting, would You help me to believe You? Would You help me believe You are who You say You are, and I am who You say I am? Would you continue to fill my mind with Your thoughts so I can agree with You? I need You, oh how I need You!"

**DECLARATION**

Jesus, I choose to stay *in* You no matter what comes my way to stir doubts and fears. You are my refuge and strong tower. You and You alone are the Truth I want to believe and have for the foundation of my life.

## "Why do you look at the speck that is in your brother's eye, but do not notice the log that is in your own eye?"

*Now He also spoke a parable to them: "A person who is blind cannot guide another who is blind, can he? Will they not both fall into a pit? A student is not above the teacher; but everyone, when he has been fully trained, will be like his teacher.* **Why do you look at the speck that is in your brother's eye, but do not notice the log that is in your own eye?** *How can you say to your brother, 'Brother, let me take out the speck that is in your eye,' when you yourself do not see the log that is in your own eye? You hypocrite, first take the log out of your own eye, and then you will see clearly to take out the speck that is in your brother's eye. For there is no good tree that bears bad fruit, nor, on the other hand, a bad tree that bears good fruit. For each tree is known by its own fruit. For people do not gather figs from thorns, nor do they pick grapes from a briar bush. The good person out of the good treasure of his heart brings forth what is good; and the evil person out of the evil treasure brings forth what is evil; for his mouth speaks from that which fills his heart* (Luke 6:39-45).

While there are several good questions asked in this parable, let's journal about the possibility of a "log" in our eye that hinders the journey of healing (verse 41).

What is the first thought that comes to your mind when you hear Jesus asking you this question today? How would you fill in these blanks?

"\_\_\_\_\_ (Your name), why do you look at the speck that is in \_\_\_\_\_'s eye, but don't notice the log that is in your own eye?"

PAL: "Lord Jesus, who am I judging? How have I judged \_\_\_\_\_?"
Would You please forgive me for judging \_\_\_\_\_ by thinking/saying they are \_\_\_\_\_? I am so sorry for judging them in this way. I would rather think

about them the way that You do. What are You thinking about _____ today so I can choose that way to think?" Listen and journal.

PAL: "Lord Jesus, as I was judging _____, what sin was I ignoring in my life? What is hindering me from seeing like You see?" Listen and journal.

## PRAYER

"Lord Jesus, thank You for helping me see the "log" in my eye. I need to be able to see like You see on my journey into wholeness. And thank You for a new way to think about _____ instead of judging them. Continue to search my heart and wash away all the debris that hinders clear vision. I love You."

## DECLARATION

Lord Jesus, with Your help I will ask You how You see people and situations before I make an assumption or judgment about them. I want to think like You think!

# APPENDIX C:

## *Christ in Me Is...*

The Creator of all Things (Colossians 1:16)

Holding all Things Together (Colossians 1:17)

The Head of the Church (Colossians 1:18)

The Alpha and Omega (Revelation 1:8, 22:13)

The Reconciler of all Things in Heaven and on Earth (Colossians 1:20)

My Peace (Ephesians 2:14)

My Strength (Philippians 4:13)

My Portion (Psalm 119:57)

My Deliverer (Romans 11:26)

My Provider (1 Timothy 6:17)

My Healer (Luke 4:23)

The Great I AM (John 8:58)

The Bread of Life (John 6:35)

The Source of all Life (John 11:25, 14:6)

My Life (Colossians 3:4)

The Light of the World (John 1:1-9, 8:12, 9:5)

My Redeemer (Job 19:25, Isaiah 59:20, 1 Corinthians 1:30)

The Lifter of my Head (Psalm 3:3)

The Word (John 1:1, 14; Revelation 19:13)

The Source of all the Treasures of Wisdom and Knowledge
(Colossians 2:3)

The Embodiment of the Fullness of the Godhead (Colossians 1:19)

The Author and Perfecter of my Faith (Hebrews 12:1)

ALL and IN ALL (Colossians 3:11)

My Advocate (1 John 2:1)

The Almighty (Revelation 1:8)

The Anointed One (Psalm 2:2, Daniel 9:25, Acts 4:25)

The High Priest (Hebrews 3:1)

My Banner (Isaiah 11:10, 12)

My Salvation (Luke 2:29-32)

The Bridegroom (Matthew 9:15, 25:1-13; John 3:29)

The Cornerstone (Matthew 21:42, 1 Peter 2:7)

The Good Shepherd (1 Peter 5:4, John 10:11)

The Chosen One (Isaiah 42:1, Luke 23:35)

The Christ (Matthew 1:16, 16:20, Mark 14:16, Luke 2:11, John 1:41,
Acts 5:42)

The Lord (Luke 6:46, Acts 2:36, Romans 10:13)

The Great Physician (Luke 4:23, Matthew 9:12)

Eternal Life (1 John 5:20)

Everlasting Father (Isaiah 9:6)

Wonderful Counselor (Isaiah 9:6)

Prince of Peace (Isaiah 9:6)

The Exact Representation of God (Hebrews 1:3)

Faithful and True (Revelation 19:11)

Faithful Witness (Revelation 1:5)

My Foundation (1 Corinthians 3:11)

Friend of Sinners (Matthew 11:19)

Gift of God (John 4:10, 2 Corinthians 9:15)

Glory of the Lord (Isaiah 40:5)

The Heir of all Things (Hebrews 1:2)

The Holy One of God (Psalm 16:10, Mark 1:24, John 6:69, Acts 2:27)

Wisdom of God (1 Corinthians 1:23)

Our Righteousness (1 Corinthians 1:30)

Our Holiness (1 Corinthians 1:30)

Our Hope (1 Timothy 1:1)

Our Hope of Glory (Colossians 1:27)

Immanuel (Isaiah 7:14, Matthew 1:23)

The King of Kings (Revelation 17:14, 19:16; 1 Timothy 6:15)

The King over all the Earth (Zechariah 14:9)

The Lamb of God (John 1:29, 1:36; Revelation 5:6-13, 6:1, 17:14, 21:22, 22:1)

The Living One (Revelation 1:18)

The Living Stone (1 Peter 2:4)

The Lord of All (Acts 10:36, Romans 12:12)

The Lord of Glory (1 Corinthians 2:8)

The Lord of Lords (Revelation 17:14, 19:16; 1 Timothy 6:15)

The Lord of the Sabbath (Matthew 12:8)

Son of Man (John 12:34)

Man of Sorrows (Isaiah 53:3)

The Master (Matthew 23:8)

Our Mediator (1 Timothy 2:5, Hebrews 8:6, 9:15, 12:24)

Our Intercessor (Romans 8:34, Hebrews 7:25)

The Bright and Morning Star (Revelation 22:16)

The Messiah (John 1:41, 4:25)

The One Who Is, Was and Is to Come (Revelation 1:4, 8)

The One Who Baptizes us with the Holy Spirit (Mark 1:7-8)

The Only Begotten Son of the Father (John 1:14, 3:16; 1 John 4:9)

The Radiance of God's Glory (Hebrews 1:3)

A Ransom for Us All (1 Timothy 2:5-6)

Our Refiner (Malachi 3:3)

The Resurrection (John 11:25)

The Righteous Judge (Acts 10:42, 2 Timothy 4:8)

The Righteous One (Acts 3:14, 7:52, 22:14; 1 John 2:1)

The Rock (1 Corinthians 10:4, 1 Peter 2:8)

The Ruler of God's Creation (Revelation 3:14)

Our Savior (Luke 2:11, John 4:42, Acts 5:31, 13:23; 2 Timothy 1:10,
    Titus 2:13, 2 Peter 1:11)

The Teacher (Matthew 19:16, 23:10, John 11:28, 13:13)

The Truth (John 14:6)

The Vine (John 15:1)

The Way (John 14:6)

# APPENDIX D:

## *In Christ...*

I am His possession (Deuteronomy 4:20, 7:6, 26:18; Exodus 19:5, 1 Peter 2:9).

I am a royal priesthood (Exodus 19:6, 1 Peter 2:9).

I am alive to God (Romans 6:11).

All grace abounds towards me (2 Corinthians 9:8).

All sufficiency is in me through Him (2 Corinthians 3:5, Philippians 4:19, Colossians 1:15-20).

I am anointed (1 John 2:20, 27, 2 Corinthians 1:21).

I am the apple of God's eye (Zechariah 2:8, Psalm 17:8).

As He is, so are we on this earth (1 John 4:17).

I am baptized into one Spirit (1 Corinthians 12:13).

I am baptized into Christ and His death (Romans 6:1-4).

I am being protected (John 10:28-30, 2 Thessalonians 3:3, Deuteronomy 31:6, Psalm 46:1).

I am loved (Romans 1:7, 5:8, 8:37-39, Ephesians 2:4-5, 1 Thessalonians 1:4, Zephaniah 3:17).

I am blameless in His sight (Colossians 1:22, Ephesians 1:4, 5:27).

I am blessed with all spiritual blessings (Ephesians 1:3).

I have comfort and bold access to the throne of God (Hebrews 4:16, 10:19).

I am born again of God (John 3:3, 1 John 5:18, 1 Peter 1:23).

I am bold as a lion (Proverbs 28:1).

I am part of the Bride of Christ (Ephesians 5:27, 2 Corinthians 11:2, John 3:29).

I was buried with Christ in His death (Romans 6:4, Colossians 2:12).

I can do all things in Christ (Philippians 4:13).

I am chosen (Col 3:12, Ephesians 1:4).

I am part of a chosen generation (1 Peter 2:9).

Christ indwells me with all his fullness (Colossians 1:19, 2:9; Ephesians 3:17).

I am a co-heir with Christ (Galatians 4:7, Romans 8:17).

I was created for good works (Ephesians 2:10).

I am curse-free (Galatians 3:13, Romans 8:2).

I am dead to sin (Romans 6:6-11, Colossians 3:3, 2 Timothy 2:11).

I have died with Christ (Colossians 2:20).

I am raised with Christ (Colossians 3:1, Ephesians 2:6-7, Romans 6:4).

I am declared holy (Colossians 1:22, 1 Corinthians 6:11, 1 Peter 1:16).

I am a disciple of Jesus (Matthew 28:19, Luke 14:27, Acts 26:28).

I am enriched (in all knowledge) (1 Corinthians 1:5, 2 Corinthians 9:11).

I belong to God (Philippians 3:12).

I am faithful (1 Timothy 1:12, Revelation 2:10, Galatians 5:22-23).

I am a fellow-citizen (Ephesians 2:19).

I am free (John 8:36, Galatians 5:1, Acts 13:38-39, Luke 4:18).

I am free from sin (Romans 6:22, 8:1-4).

He has freely given me all things (Romans 8:32, 1 Corinthians 2:12, 2 Peter 1:3).

I am a friend of Christ (John 15:13, 15).

I am fruitful (John 15:5).

I am gifted (1 Corinthians 7:7).

I am a habitation of God (Ephesians 2:22).

I have the mind of Christ (1 Corinthians 2:16, Philippians 2:5).

God is at work in me (Philippians 1:6, 2:13).

He is for me, not against me (Romans 8:31, Psalm 118:6).

I am healed (1 Peter 2:24, Isaiah 53:4, Psalm 103:1-5).

I am hidden in Christ (Colossians 3:3).

I am highly favored (Ephesians 1:3, 3 John 1:2, Proverbs 10:22).

We are His body (1 Corinthians 12:27, Romans 12:5).

I am His workmanship (Ephesians 2:10).

We are a holy nation (1 Peter 2:9).

I am increasing in the knowledge of God (Colossians 1:10, 2 Peter 3:18).

I am inseparable from the love of God (Romans 8:35-39).

I am justified (Romans 5:1, Galatians 2:16).

The Kingdom of God is within me (Luke 17:20-21).

I am known by Him (1 Corinthians 8:3, 13:12).

I am lacking in nothing (Psalm 23:1, James 1:4).

I am the light of the world (Matthew 5:14-16).

I am living and walking by faith (2 Corinthians 5:7, Galatians 2:20, Hebrews 11:6).

I live by God's Word (Psalm 86:11, Matthew 4:4, John 8:31-32, Ephesians 6:17).

I am a living stone (1 Peter 2:5).

I am made in His image (Genesis 1:27).

I am made rich in everything (2 Corinthians 9:11, 6:10).

I am more than a conqueror (Romans 8:37, 1 Corinthians 15:57, 1 John 5:4).

I am a new creation (2 Corinthians 5:17).

I have a sound mind (2 Timothy 1:7).

I am ordained (John 15:16, Ephesians 2:10).

I am a different person (1 Peter 2:9, Colossians 3:10, 2 Corinthians 3:18).

I am purified (1 John 3:3, Hebrews 10:22, Ephesians 2:1-22).

I am filled with resurrection life (Philippians 3:10, Colossians 1:29, Galatians 2:20, Ephesians 3:17).

I am redeemed (Colossians 1:14, Isaiah 43:1, Ephesians 1:7, Romans 3:24-26).

I am the righteousness of God (2 Corinthians 5:21, Romans 3:21-31).

I am a saint (Ephesians 1:18, 2 Peter 1:4).

I am the salt of the earth (Matthew 5:13).

I am sanctified (1 Thessalonians 5:23-24, 2 Thessalonians 2:13, 1 Corinthians 1:30, 6:11; Hebrews 10:10).

I am saved (Acts 16:31, Romans 10:9-10, John 3:16, 10:28-30; Ephesians 2:8, Hebrews 7:25).

I am seated with Him in heavenly places (Ephesians 2:6-7).

I am a servant of God (John 12:26, 13:12-15; Philippians 2:5-8, 1 Corinthians 4:1).

I share His authority (Matthew 16:19, Mark 11:23, Luke 10:19, John 14:12, Acts 1:8, 1 John 4:4).

I am a sheep of His pasture (Psalm 95:7, 100:3; Ezekiel 34:31).

I am a shining star (Philippians 2:15).

I am a son of God (Galatians 3:26, 4:6-7; John 1:12, Romans 8:14-16, 2 Corinthians 6:18, 1 John 3:1-2).

I am a son of light (1 Thessalonians 5:5, Ephesians 5:8, John 12:36).

I am a steward of the mysteries (1 Corinthians 4:1).

I am strengthened by Him (Philippians 4:13, Ephesians 3:16, Colossians 1:11, 2 Corinthians 12:9-10, Isaiah 40:29, 31).

I am the fullness of life and godliness (2 Peter 1:3, Colossians 2:9, John 1:16, Romans 15:29, Ephesians 1:23, 3:19).

I am the temple of God (1 Corinthians 3:16-17, 6:19).

I am a vessel of glory (2 Corinthians 3:18, Romans 9:23).

I am a vessel of honor (Romans 9:21, 2 Timothy 2:21).

I am a citizen of Heaven (Philippians 3:20).

I am a slave of righteousness (Romans 6:18).

I walk in newness of life (Romans 6:4).

I am a warrior (Psalm 18:39, 44:5; Ephesians 6:10-18).

I am wise (Psalm 37:30, 1 Corinthians 1:30, James 1:5).

I am a witness (Matthew 5:16, Acts 1:8, 4:20, 22:15; Romans 1:16, 1 Peter 3:15).

I am an ambassador for Christ (2 Corinthians 5:20).

I am forgiven (Matthew 6:14-15, Ephesians 1:7, Colossians 1:14, 3:13).

# APPENDIX E:

## *The Five "Rs" Activation*

The Five "Rs" are:

- Recognize the lie you have believed and on which you have based your life.

- Repent for believing the lie. Ask the Holy Spirit to help you write a Godly belief.

- Renew your mind according to this fresh insight from God through:

- Repetition and

- Rehearsal

Take your time recognizing the lie and praying the *Prayer of Recognition and Repentance* referenced in this appendix.

We first began to *recognize* we needed help because we were stuck in an unhealthy pattern. We either recognized the behavior(s), the feeling(s) or the thought(s) that were destructive – and the resulting fruit.

Although some teach that you have to identify your feelings or behavior before you can change, I have come to believe that while you can start with identifying those key elements in your life, you will also need to identify the lie that you are believing to be true in order to have lasting change.

*Repentance* means to change the way you think so you can change the way you live. The fruit of repentance is changed behavior. Scripture says to be transformed by the way we think (Romans 12:2). It also says, "As a man thinks in his heart, that is the way he is" (Proverbs 27:3).

Here are some great questions to PAL as you identify a lie or ungodly belief: "Lord, I have been living my life based on a belief that leads me to express emotions negatively and to act based on those emotions. The results are not good fruit. What have I been thinking to be true that leads to those negatively expressed emotions? I feel _____ (negatively expressed emotions) because I think _____. What would You like to say to me about this belief/thought? What would You like me to think instead? Where in Scripture would You like me to read so I can think more like You?"

When we repent of living our life based on lies, we are agreeing with God that we have sinned against Him and are asking for Him to forgive and cleanse us according to 1 John 1:9. The following prayer is a pattern I use to pray for myself and also with others as I help facilitate the Five "Rs" Activation.

## PRAYER OF RECOGNITION AND REPENTANCE

I confess my sin of believing the lie that _____.

I forgive and release all who influenced my thought patterns as I embraced this lie. Be specific.

Lord, what consequences are working in my life as a result of living my life based on this lie? _____ I also forgive _____ for these consequences. They don't owe me anything. The record on their account is erased.

Would You please forgive me, Father, for embracing this lie, living my life based on it, and for any way I have judged others because of it? (Wait to listen to His response to you. Hearing Him tell you that you are forgiven will bring an impartation you don't want to miss as it deepens the reality of God's forgiveness.) Write down what you hear Him say or what He shows you.

Thank You for forgiving me, Father. I receive Your forgiveness.

Because You have forgiven me, I choose to let myself off the hook for believing this lie and living my life based on it. I will not continue to beat myself up over the struggles I experience(d) as a result of this lie. I agree with You, God, that I am forgiven!

I renounce and break my agreement with this lie. I now choose to embrace a Kingdom of God perspective and forsake any tie to this lie.

I choose to accept, believe and receive what You say is true, Lord. What do You want me to believe instead of this lie? What Scripture would You lead me to so I can embrace the mind of Christ? (Listen and record what He says – these words are your new weapon to defeat the old way of thinking.) God might show you a picture or give you a phrase or Scripture on which to meditate.

Take your time working through this prayer. Let it soak into your inner being, becoming a reality in you as the Holy Spirit brings transformation.

We *Renew* our minds through *Repetition* and *Rehearsal* of the truth God has spoken to us. Renewal of the mind can begin once you have a new, Godly thought to think instead of the lie. When you focus on a new thought pattern long enough, it becomes a habit. You are embracing the principle of spiritual displacement (take that off, put this on). The indwelling, super-natural presence of the Holy Spirit enables you to walk in newness of life as you embrace the process of having your mind renewed ("…be transformed by the renewing of your mind" Romans 12:2).

You are ready to begin *Repetition* of the new thought seven to twelve times a day. Say it out loud, thinking about what you are saying. As you repeat the new thought, PAL: "Holy Spirit, would You show me ways I can apply this new thought to my behavior and begin to Rehearse it – practice it? How will this new thought change my behavior?" Think about the circumstances and people with whom you have had difficulty practicing this particular skill/behavior with and intentionally apply what you have learned in each opportunity presented.

Scripture reinforces this principle in many places; here are a few of my favorite verses that relate:

> *This book of the Law shall not depart from your mouth, but you shall meditate on it day and night, so that you may be careful to do according to all that is written in it. For then you will make your way prosperous, and then you will have good success (Joshua 1:8).*

> *The word is near you, in your mouth and in your heart (that is, the word of faith that we proclaim); because, if you confess with your mouth that Jesus is Lord and believe in your heart that God raised him from the dead, you will be saved. For with the heart one believes and is justified, and with the mouth one confesses and is saved (Romans 10:8-10).*

> *For this commandment that I command you today is not too hard for you, neither is it far off. It is not in Heaven, that you should say, 'Who will ascend to Heaven for us and bring it to us, that we may hear it and do it?' Neither is it beyond the sea, that you should say, 'Who will go over the sea for us and bring it to us, that we may hear it and do it?' But the word is very near you. It is in your mouth and in your heart, so that you can do it (Deuteronomy 30:11-14).*

We may think it is too hard to change, but God says it is possible, so it is. We have to have this mindset as we begin to develop new ways of thinking. It is possible – with God's help! Otherwise He wouldn't ask us to do it!

# SUMMARY

- Recognize

- Repent

- Renew

- Repetition

- Rehearsal

# APPENDIX F:

## *Warning and Weapon Activation*

One day as I was praying with someone to help them in their journey of changing old habit patterns, the words *warning* and *weapon* dropped into my spirit. I heard the Lord say, "Ask them what their warning sign is when they are about to fall into an old way of thinking, feeling or behaving. Ask them how they know when they are about to revert to an old default system."

As I have worked with this principle, it has proved to help me and many others. I PAL: "What feelings begin to arise within that let me know I will need to choose a new way of thinking?" Or, "What negative thought pattern am I thinking that will lead me to act in a way I don't want to?" In Romans the Apostle Paul said, " Why do I do the things I don't want to do?"

I believe we can pay attention to warning signs, whether they are particular thoughts that don't agree with God or old familiar feelings we have been trying to change. Sometimes we behave in a way we don't want, and that is also a warning. We change the way we feel and act by changing the way we think.

A *warning* is an opportunity for us to pause and *PAL* to help us iden- tify what we are thinking that is allowing a negative feeling and behavior to be expressed. "Lord, what am I thinking that is making me feel _____?" Or, "When I think _____, I feel _____, then I _____ (behavior). Or, "I feel _____ because I think _____ and then I _____ (behavior)."

This is what I call "Yellow Light Theology." Several years ago I was driving and approached a yellow stoplight. As I went through the yellow light without giving it a second thought, I heard the Holy Spirit say, "Carolyn, is that how you are going to respond to Me if I caution you about slowing or stopping when you are about to let your feelings control your behavior? When I am trying to teach you to stop and evaluate your perspective to change your responses? Are you going to keep right on moving?"

In that moment, I realized that *I have a choice when it comes to my thoughts, feelings and behavior.* If I choose to go through the "yellow lights" instead of slowing or stopping, I will "do the things I don't want to do" and end up back in the cycle of defeating behaviors.

What thought, feeling or behavior helps you become aware that an old default system is about to be reactivated? We are vulnerable to these old patterns as we work toward developing new habits. We can say to them, "I recognize you. I will stop right now and renounce you. I recognize your tactics and I refuse to allow you to continue. I will use my new weapon by speaking it and releasing it as my new reality in the Kingdom. I will no longer entertain these negative feelings, thoughts or behaviors. I have no space in my head for this lie. I disown you. This is how I think now."

Renounce is a forceful word used only a few times in the Bible, depending on the translation you read. It is used in 2 Corinthians 4:2 and talks about disowning the "hidden things of shame." For most of us, the habit patterns we are trying to change have come from shameful things in our past that continue to affect our lives today. These patterns (the Bible calls them strongholds) keep us from experiencing the freedom Christ has given to us, keeping us *stuck*!

We have a short period between the time we start thinking a thought and deciding whether to meditate on it. If we decide we don't want the thought and reject it, it does not enter our long-term memory. If it does, however, we'll have a stronghold to tear down, and that takes more energy and work than if we quickly realize that the thought is not in agreement with Jesus Christ. When we agree with Jesus, we are then free to say to the ungodly thought, "You are not welcome, and I renounce you." We can immediately refocus on a Godly thought.

A familiar emotion for me is fear and anxiety when I think about provision for the future. I experience warning signs in my thoughts, feelings and behavior. My body tenses up, I feel stressed, and I start thinking of different scenarios that could happen. Some of those thoughts might be, "You won't have enough. God won't come through. You better figure this out or you will be in big trouble. Why didn't you…you sure were stupid… you should have…"

If I don't stop and realize I am in a warning phase, I will allow my mind to think all kinds of thoughts. I will make up stories in my head that will produce negative feelings, and I will spend several days, even weeks sometimes, in a grumpy, fearful, stressed out attitude. This makes me miserable and most likely those around me will be affected. Learning to recognize the warning signs that take me to old habit patterns of thought, feeling and behavior is crucial to walk in newness of life.

When we work on changing a habit pattern, we receive a new thought that agrees with God. PAL, "Lord, what weapon do You want to give me to establish this new thought so it becomes a new habit for me?" This becomes our offensive *weapon* – the specific word that God has spoken to us to replace the lie. "For the weapons of our warfare are not of the flesh but have divine power to destroy strongholds. We destroy arguments and every lofty opinion raised against the knowledge of God and take every thought captive to obey Christ" (2 Corinthians 10:4).

Our weapon might be a Bible verse, a picture God showed us, a thought or phrase, or an action He has inspired to put us on the offensive when we are tempted to live out of an old habit structure. The weapon needs to be something simple and concise so we can easily recall it and put it into practice when attacks come. 1 Peter 1:13 encourages us to prepare our minds for action. We are not to be conformed to former ways of living, but to the ways of Jesus Christ. What weapon has He given you to prepare you for any situation you will face?

I have learned to stop and say to fear, "I recognize you and your tactics, and you have no place in me. I renounce you and stand here with Jesus. Because He is here at my right hand, I will not be shaken!" The Lord spoke that verse to me from Psalm 16:8 to calm my fears, and now it is one of my life verses. It immediately brings peace to my mind and emotions. Unexpected circumstances that happen to us in our lives do not have to shake us and take us off the foundation of the life of Christ within. But we have to know our warning signs and use our weapons to take the offensive and stay in a place of agreement with God.

I now say, "I have given up fear and anxiousness for the future. I forbid you even to approach me. I will not entertain you in my thoughts." When I catch the warning sign at this stage, the feelings of fear and anxiousness aren't allowed because a new Godly thought (i.e., "Jesus is here at my right hand and I will not be shaken") is in place, and feelings of security follow.

When we learn to renounce ungodly thoughts and rehearse Godly thoughts as soon as we have a warning sign, we change the direction of our feelings and behavior. *We get to choose our feelings and behaviors.* Renounce also means to "take leave of" or forsake. We must learn to forbid old habit patterns to influence us when we have a new way to think given to us in Jesus Christ. We are now new creations and have the mind of Christ and His supernatural indwelling presence enabling us to walk in newness of life (1 Corinthians. 2:16, Philippians 2:13, 2 Corinthians. 5:17).

For every new thought we are developing as a habit, we must be aware of our warnings and our weapons and be ready to use them at a moment's notice. Don't rush past the warning signs or you will find yourself in trouble. My husband had to teach me about the warning lights on the dash of our car. Don't ignore them, he said, or you may find yourself stuck on the side of the road and have to call for emergency help. Thankfully I have not had to learn that lesson the hard way. But I have run past my emotional warning signs and found myself repeating behaviors, saying out of frustration along with the Apostle Paul, "Why do I keep doing the things I don't want to do?" (Romans 7:15)

We truly have a new nature living in us that the Holy Spirit empowers. Let's learn to live from that place as a habit (walking in the Spirit), knowing that we have the DNA of God living in us (2 Peter 1:4). We *are dead* to sin. We *are alive* to God in Christ Jesus. We *have grace* to walk in newness of life! (Romans 6:11)

What is your warning sign? What is your weapon of choice when the warning sign goes off?

## SUMMARY

- Know your *warning* sign. What thought, feeling or behavior are you about to reactivate that pulls you back into your old nature?

- Know your *weapon*. What has God given you to go on the offensive against this specific lie?

# ENDNOTES

1   Heartland Church is a neighborhood congregation that is growing a regional church with an international reach. Heartland was founded in 1985 as part of the Vineyard Movement by Pastors Ron and Carolyn Allen. It is a three-streams expression of the body of Christ that now belongs to the Anglican Church of North America.

2   Rev. Dr. Carolyn R. Allen, *Journey into Wholeness*, (Fort Wayne, Indiana, 2017). Available on amazon.com.

3   Marilee Adams, *The Art of the Question: A Guide to Short-Term Question-Centered Therapy*, (John Wiley & Sons, Inc. Publishing, New York, 1998). Preface.

4   Albert Einstein. amorebeautifulquestion.com. https://amorebeautifulquestion.com/einstein-questioning/

5   Dr. Mark Virkler, *4 Keys to Hearing God's Voice*, www.CWGMinistries.org/4keys

6   Ibid.

7   Albert Einstein. amorebeautifulquestion.com. https://amorebeautifulquestion.com/einstein-questioning/

8   Martin B. Copenhaver, *Jesus Is The Question*, (Abingdon Press, 2014), 20.

9   Dr. Caroline Leaf, *Who Switched Off My Brain*, (Southlake, TX: Thomas Nelson Pub, 2009), Chapters 1 and 2.

10  Marilee Adams, Ph.D., *Change Your Questions, Change Your Life*, (San Francisco, CA: Berrett-Koehler Pub. Inc., 2009), 87.

11    Caroline Leaf. Switch On Your Brain Quotes: The Key to Peak Happiness, Thinking, and Health. Goodreads.com. https://www.goodreads.com/work/quotes/26928437-switch-on-your-brain-the-key-to-peak-happiness-thinking-and-health?page=3

12    Ibid.

13    Edward De Bono.InquiryInstitute.com, 2009. https://inquiryinstitute.com/resources/question-quotes/

14    Dr. Caroline Leaf, *Who Switched Off My Brain*, (Southlake, TX: Thomas Nelson Pub, 2009), Chapters 1 and 2.

15    Caroline Leaf, Switch On Your Brain Quotes: The Key to Peak Happiness, Thinking, and Health. Goodreads,com. https://www.goodreads.com/work/quotes/26928437-qswitch-on-your-brain-the-key-to-peak-happiness-thinking-and-health?page=3

16    Charles Kettering Quotes. BrainyQuote.com, BrainyMedia Inc, 2021. https://www.brainyquote.com/quotes/charles kettering 181210.

17    Dr. Mark Virkler, www.cwgministries.org/\

18    Doug Savage. GoComics.com, ©2013. https://www.gocomics.com/savagechickens/2017/09/01

19    For our purposes, I define "declaration" as a proclamation based on the Word of God spoken boldly with the intent of taking action. Declarations direct our lives toward what we say (James 3:4-5). "Words kill, words give life; they are either poison or fruit – you choose" (Proverbs 18:21 MSG). Words can move us toward experiencing all for which Jesus died. "For by your words you will be justified and by your words you will be condemned" (Matthew 12:37). Paraphrasing also helps make a declaration personal when using Scripture. In the text, I paraphrased Psalm 16:8. Also, see Introduction to Appendices B through D.